D0279824

THE ANNALS OF BALLYKILFERRET

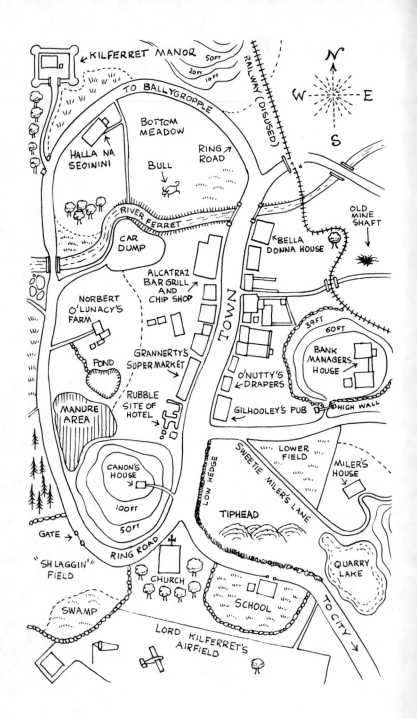

FRANK KELLY

THE ANNALS OF BALLYKILFERRET

Illustrated by Terry Willers

Gill and Macmillan

First published 1979 by
Gill and Macmillan Ltd
15/17 Eden Quay
Dublin 1
with associated companies in
London, New York, Delhi, Hong Kong, Johannesburg,
Lagos, Melbourne, Singapore, Tokyo

Typeset by Joe Healy Typesetting, Dublin
Printed in Great Britain by
Richard Clay (The Chaucer Press) Ltd.
Bungay, Suffolk.

THE skeletal trees thrust stark black fingers of scorn at the grey rain-laden sky, and with every urgent gust of wind the rooks rose in a black spiral of angry ragged cawing. They looked down on the town of Ballykilferret, its one thoroughfare worthy of the name street clinging like the suckling young of some worm-like and long-extinct animal to the low hill beyond the trees.

Ballykilferret, raped and put to the flame by the Danes, dragged unwilling into marriage by the Normans, and systematically sodomised by a long line of English gentry and troops, learned, like the whores of Europe, to service the current army of occupation and, when they departed, the conquerors were left wondering who had really screwed whom.

The people of Ballykilferret have always shown an ability to adapt to change. Within days of the first handshake be-

tween Diarmuid McMurrough and the first Norman lord to arrive on Irish soil, a small ferrety runner was seen heading for the coast, his mission to offer the overlordship of Ballykilferret together with the undying sycophancy of its inhabitants.

The first Norman lord of the area, one Hugo de Kilferret, was met on the outskirts of the town by the local chief, O Lubhnasa Maol, or the bald O'Lunacy, his emaciated figure prostrate in the dust of a hot summer's day, bald bullet head face-down and skinny legs with knotted varicose veins protruding at either end of a mangey moulting goatskin. This was to be the keynote of the relationship between the O'Lunacys and the de Kilferret family for generations, until the de Kilferrets merged with the later English stock, who took for granted the relationship of posterior to toilet paper between themselves and the O'Lunacys.

The baldness of O Lubhnasa Maol was attributed to early experiments in the brewing of certain local spiritous liquors, which were said to have caused the loss of his hair in one glorious hallucinatory night. But, as it was put even then in Ballykilferret, 'people would say anything to make mischief'.

The haughty admonishment to the O Lubhnasa Maol to rise from the dust and not to be making an utter eejit of himself was somewhat marred by the O Lubhnasa Maol's total inability to understand the Norman tongue, and the resulting impasse had such a traumatic effect on the choleric Norman lord that his first administrative act in the area was the issuing of an edict that the use of the Irish language was to cease forthwith under pain of horrific penalties, to be announced within the week.

The announcement was never made, however, as the entire population of Ballykilferret to a man, was speaking a mixture of pidgin Norman French and the English of the time within three days, such was its ability to adapt to change.

The resulting cacophony was so painful to the ear that the old lord, to save what was left of his dwindling sanity, opted for their speaking English alone, preferring that they should lacerate the English language rather than his own.

Thus, the inhabitants of Ballykilferret were in the peculiar position of having abandoned their native tongue with such rapidity and finality, that all they had left of it was the 'Blás' or accents of it, with no memory of the original Irish language. This resulted in the emergence of a phenomenon peculiar to the area, the existence of a sort of language without words known just as 'the Blás'. To this day the Ballykilferret people can be heard exchanging these sounds in the course of their daily commerce, but asked to tell their meaning they would be quite unable to explain themselves.

There has always been a strong bond between the overlords of the area and the local inhabitants, and this was a source of considerable prosperity to the town for several hundred years.

Prior to the coming of Irish independence, there was no local tradition of rebellion against the reigning powers, unlike other areas of Ireland. Thus, during the sporadic outbreaks of unrest throughout the country's troubled history it was not uncommon for information to be given to the authorities about men 'on the run' by the Ballykilferret people.

Considerable sums of money were paid for this information, and in time the practice of 'informin'' became quite a thriving local industry.

There is an old saying in the area which runs: 'A word spoke is a secret broke, and a secret broke is money in the pocket'. The tradition of 'informin' gave rise to many ballads such as the famous 'Redcoats Abú!', and 'Bould Oliver Cromwell, The Darlin' of Erin', which are still to be heard at local festive gatherings.

The singers of these ballads bear certain distinguishing facial marks, such as split lips and disfigured eyebrow and jaw lines, acquired when they encountered adverse responses to their art in public houses outside the area. It is often said with some pride of a local bard that he is 'a great man to lie down under blows'.

The people of Ballykilferret have in common what can only be described by the metaphysical term, 'Ballykilferretness'. It isn't that they all look alike, although a low hairline and forehead with bushy eyebrows are not uncommon, neither are a shortness of stature and prominence of the lower jaw, the latter giving a misleading air of determination to its bearers.

No, it's just that, in the words of the Matron of the Cottage

3

Hospital, who has always made it clear that, despite her long service, she is definitely not a native of the area, 'there is a look'.

Perhaps this is best illustrated by a case which was heard before a visiting judge on circuit in which a witness claimed that he had been assaulted by a group of men outside a dance hall on a dark night. There was some confusion about the identity of the assailants and the witness was asked to be more specific in his description of them.

His reply was, that although he couldn't be quite sure that the accused were the men who had administered the blows to his person they were probably the culprits, as his attackers were 'Ballykilferret men by the look of them'.

This description went no small way towards bringing about the conviction of the accused, an example no doubt of how a little local knowledge can be of assistance to a judge in applying the absolute justice of the law.

Just as many creatures seem to have the chameleon-like capacity of acquiring something of the appearance of their surroundings, it might be stated conversely that Ballykilferret is a place which is, like its inhabitants, low and bushy-browed.

The low grey-brown hills of the area are fringed with wind-seared trees which are a heartening example of the power of growing things to surmount the despotic capriciousness of nature. These trees, beech and oak alike, have evolved rugged, stocky constitutions, and although of low stature in comparison to their counterparts in other localities, they survive while their taller and finer-grained brothers are toppled by the winter gales.

Similarly, the houses of Ballykilferret are built close to the ground, but, surprisingly, they are distinguished by a remarkable prodigality of windows. The penal days of window tax, of such unhappy memory throughout Ireland, stirred into life the inventive genius of the people of Ballykilferret in a most intriguing way.

Ever demonstrative of their capacity to adapt to adverse conditions, the local people devised a form of detachable window frame which could be speedily removed from its setting and replaced by a mud-bonded grouping of stones, the whole topped off inside and out by large roughly-cut and white-washed flakes of rock, so completing the camouflage.

Thus, on the day of assessment of the dreaded window tax, the unfortunate official assigned to the task was confronted with a bewildering paucity of taxable apertures, and departed sadly to report meagre prospects of revenue from this source to his masters.

The departure of the official was generally followed by wild scenes of rejoicing at the success of the deception, the local people dancing around bonfires to the accompaniment of céilí music and the imbibing of the local brew.

On one such occasion, however, the official's horse went lame shortly after he had departed from the town, causing him to return unexpectedly after the celebrations had begun. Had he been particularly astute, he might have noticed the barely perceptible slackening of the tempo, or the fact that the dancers exchanged meaningful glances in an inkling while twirling to the wild music, but the poor man could find no explanation for his sudden involvement in the dance or the fact that every time there was a lull in the activities he discovered a glassful of clear and fiery liquid in his hand.

It was with even greater bewilderment that he found himself in the vice-like grip of the legs of the postmistress in a haybarn later in the evening, and as he clung grimly to her grey bun, dimly aware of the pain of a hairpin piercing his hand and the wing of her steel spectacles cutting into his temple as he came to a reluctant climax, he little thought that there was such frenzied replacing of windows taking place throughout the town.

As he rode out of Ballykilferret the following mid-day on a borrowed and moulting mount, every movement of the bony, hollow-backed animal wreaking ecstacies of pain in his throbbing head and increasing the sensation of warm weakness between his legs, he noted with satisfaction that his first calculations had been correct, and put the previous evening's blurred and fleeting impression of many windows down to the effects of the dancing and the drink.

'Good God ye'll never learn', he chided himself. 'At your age ye ought to have more sense'.

'Still', he thought smugly, 'ye didn't know ye had that

5

little shot left in yer locker', and the children who peeped at him unseen from behind the weeds in the ditches wondered why the stranger was smiling to himself.

Finding the exact location of Ballykilferret consists more of acquiring a way of thinking than of following specific directions. In the words of the Nod Rooney, a renowned sage of the area, 'ye lave the Irish Sea at yer back at Dublin, head north-west lavin' Lough Owel on yer left, and that's the last sea ye'll see 'till ye see Ballykilferret'.

One intrepid traveller, having found the town by chance and spent a few pleasant days there, asked the Nod for the most direct route to be followed back to Dublin, only to be met with the reply: 'Ah well, if ye were lookin' for a direct route back to Dublin, Ballykilferret wouldn't be the place to start at all'.

AT one time it was feared that the cultural heritage of the Blás might die out, but with the emergence of modern Irish nationalism in the form of grants by successive governments of considerable sums of money for the preservation of the national culture there was a remarkable resurgence of an interest in the Blás.

Evidence of this are the annual Blás competitions which are held in the local hall in Ballykilferret, Halla na Seoiníní, where the bards and poets of Ballykilferret suspend their daily devouring interest in the game of pool to submit Blás 'poems without words' and Blás songs for audition by a panel of judges. The selected entries are performed in the evening time before the local inhabitants and the occasional hardy visiting cultural devotee, to the accompaniment of harsh cries of encouragement and the traditional barrage of missiles from the audience.

The onus is on the performer to survive the rain of objects, many of them testing his artistic sensitivity to the limit by odour and by content, as well as such sabotage as the pulling of the microphone plug at intervals throughout the performance. Any show of discomfiture at these distractions results in the immediate disqualification by acclamation of the competitor.

One unfortunate unsuccessful entrant in a recent competition, who weakened to the extent of calling the assembled gathering 'a pack of bloody lousers', was immediately expelled horizontally from the hall by dozens of pairs of willing hands. One wonders at the continuing existence of such competitions, but still the grants go on, and still the competitions continue.

It is argued that the Blás keeps alive a valuable sense of community, and indeed this may well be so. It is to be noted

7

that intrusion by alien cultural influences is frequently countered by use of the Blás. Thus when confronted by a question from a visitor to the area which might demand the revelation of local information (always jealously guarded), the inhabitants are frequently heard to break into use of the Blás among themselves until the visitor wearies of his quest and goes on his way unanswered.

The powerhouse of ideas and energy behind Ballykilferret's cultural activities and tourism is one Gubnet O'Lunacy, direct descendant of O Lubhnasa Maol and initiator of Ballykilferret's Fertilizer Festival and Festival of Weeds.

The idea for the former dawned on Gubnet as he surveyed the havoc wrought by the cattle on the town's street at the end of a fair day. Other towns celebrated their own characteristic features, why not Ballykilferret? A committee was formed and various names were suggested for a festival, including the Ballykilferret Manure Festival.

This was overruled by a faction headed by the Bank Manager's Wife, however, as being 'impolite', and in the ensuing argument suggestions were made which could not be repeated in this account.

Finally it was agreed that the festival should be called the Fertilizer Festival, although the Bank Manager's Wife insisted that it should be recorded in the minutes that she had approved the title with reluctance.

Interest in the Fertilizer Festival dwindled, to the immense satisfaction of that formidable woman, when it became apparent that the central tourism body in Dublin was unwilling to cough up the customary financial aid for a festival with such a challenging title.

However, one should not underrate the ingenuity and resourcefulness of a man of the calibre of Gubnet O'Lunacy. It was while helping the Gardaï in their enquiries in connection with matters surrounding the proposed visit of a tax inspector to the locality that Gubnet happened to read a printed warning against harbouring certain noxious weeds, such as barbary ragwort, dock and thistles, which was attached to a notice board in the Garda Station. In the course of this historic perusal, the idea for the Festival of Weeds was born.

Having dismissed the idea of electing a 'Miss Forklift', it

was decided to choose a 'Queen of the Ragwort', and to honour this elevated damsel by having her picture published in the *Ballykilferret Bugle*. The festival had interesting accompanying events such as a long-distance spitting contest, a 'shlaggin'' competition and foot-tripping competition.

This last event proved to be the most popular with the local youths. There was an attractive freedom of expression about it, deriving from the fact that there were no actual rules, and it depended on the native opportunism of the sons of Ballykilferret.

The sudden removal of the legs from under an unsuspecting, parcel-laden citizen became a common sight in the town, accompanied by whoops of triumph from the stealthy assailant. Finally the Bank Manager had the legs taken from under him, and that put an end to the foot-tripping competition.

The incident involving the Bank Manager brought a temporary lull in Ballykilferret's festival fever, but Gubnet was undaunted. The committee was galvanised by his next ingenious suggestion. Why not have an all-the-year-round festival? What a wonderful idea! The festival could be allowed to sleep or stirred into life to meet Ballykilferret's fluctuating tourism needs.

On one memorable occasion when the Garda Sergeant's brother was home from America on a short holiday, there was free hand-balling in the alley, and all the ivy was scraped off it for this attraction of the temporarily revived festival.

The climax of the week's festivities was a concert held in Halla na Seoiníní, which featured a comedian from the neighbouring parish of Ballygropple.

It is a generally accepted fact that any stand-up comedian must overcome a certain amount of audience resistance before he wins the indulgence of his listeners, but in Ballykilferret the comedy performer's task is one of unparalleled formidableness. As it is sometimes said in Ballykilferret, 'the local lads doesn't take too kindly to jokes'.

The news of the arrival of this exhaulted Thespian from Ballygropple travelled among the youth of Ballykilferret by some mysterious telegraph with the speed of lightning. Indeed, had he looked up from the sumptuous pile of ham and tomatoes which was engaging his attention in the canon's house shortly after his arrival, he would have seen many pairs

9

of eyes peering at him from behind the shrubs and bushes of the reverend gentleman's garden.

The explorers who first encountered some of the world's most primitive inhabitants in the jungles of the Amazon Basin must have met the same expression of implacable hostility in the eyes of their stone-age brothers as might have been seen by the comedian, had he not been under the canon's housekeeper's culinary spell.

But perhaps the fates were merciful in providing the diner with a limboesque sense of security before undergoing the ordeal of the concert.

His first joke was greeted with the kind of silence which must have existed in the tomb of Tutankhamun before its long slumber was invaded by the first intruders. As it was put by the Nod Rooney, 'the joke went down like an erection in a heart attack'.

His next few efforts to entertain the audience were met with the same disheartening reaction, or indeed lack of it. Bewildered, he paused in his divine flow, thinking that perhaps he was alone in his ignorance of some appalling cataclysm, of which his audience was already aware.

The silence had a terrifying animal palpability which caused the hair to rise on the back of the performer's neck and forearms. He felt as the victim must feel at the moment of truth in a cabalistic ritual involving human sacrifice.

Suddenly there was a cry, terrifying in its aloneness in the empty ether, 'Get up the yard ye silly bollocks, yer flies is open!' This was immediately followed by harsh demoniacal cackles of laughter.

He didn't remember his flight from the stage, or his passage down the back stairs of the hall past dusty scenic mementoes of former theatrical glories in Ballykilferret. Indeed he was pedalling hard well beyond the borders of the parish when he discovered that his tormentors had let the wind out of his bicycle tyres.

Despite what this scion of Ballygropple may have thought, the concert was considered 'a thunderin' success' by the youth of Ballykilferret, so much so that the committee issued an invitation to the victim to perform again in the next concert. Who knows what hysterical acts of homage lay in store for him had he had the temerity to accept the invitation. As a result of his refusal he was described as 'yella like all before him from that muck-heap of a parish'.

Following the success of the concert, there sprang from the inexhaustible well of Gubnet O'Lunacy's mind the concept of incorporating a song contest in the All-The-Year-Round Festival.

While surveying the original excremental inspiration for the first festival, Gubnet was running through his mind the immortal lines of William Butler Yeats about the town of Collooney in Sligo, 'A small church with a big steeple, a small town with a proud people'. Suddenly he found himself murmuring, 'A small town with a strong pong, a small town with no song!'

Favourable reaction to the song contest was unanimous, and there was feverish activity among lyricists and arrangers, resulting in such memorable entries as 'Cheek To Cheek', 'When I Take My Sugar To Tea' and 'Can't Help Lovin' That Man Of Mine'.

When it was pointed out to Gubnet that these titles had a somewhat familiar ring to them, the critic was met with: 'They're new down here, whatever about where you come from'.

Fate dealt the cards in a strange way for the choice of the winning entry in the song contest. An extension of the drinking hours was required for the festival, and the District Justice was showing some reluctance to grant this permission, deemed vital to the success of the festivities.

The committee members were pondering this problem when Gubnet O'Lunacy discovered among the pile of songs, one which had been entered by the District Justice. Suddenly it dawned upon the committee that this song showed unparalleled originality in lyrics and tune. This was the kind of entry which justified the existence of the contest. If the contest could bring to light such creative fire, and send forth such musical joys to delight countless generations to come, then the efforts of everyone involved would be worthwhile.

So great was the excitement caused by the discovery of the song that a messenger was sent hot-foot to the District Justice to tell him the glad tidings of his success in the contest. The application for an extension of the drinking hours was granted the following morning.

11

THE increased availability of drink created an ambience highly favourable to the 'shlaggin' competition. 'Shlaggin', which can best be described as a sort of prolonged verbal duelling, is a fiercely competitive activity, which can take place in any given place at any given time, but there are also formal 'shlaggin' tournaments with grand finals, held in traditional venues.

A 'shlaggin' match can develop quite spontaneously. Two drinkers might be perched side by side on bar stools at a pub counter for an hour or more, when suddenly one of them might say: 'Begob you're the man that has all the money. I'd say ye'd know a fiver if ye saw one'. Another hour of silence might elapse before the other would reply: 'Get hup ya boy ya!'

The author of the latter profundity would be aware that he was the loser of this encounter, but he might have to wait two or three weeks for his revenge. Opportunities for 'shlaggin' may not be grabbed gratuitously, but must have an organic development. Thus the victor might be working with some colleagues hauling muck or mending fencing at the roadside, when the loser would arrive on the scene and pull up in his tractor for 'a bit of a chat'. Lulled into a false sense of security by the proferred cigarette and the pleasantly acrid convivial smoke, and the apparently relaxed chat of his former victim, he would be suddenly met with the frontal assault of: 'Muck is right, and well for them that has it!' He would then know that the 'shlag' was 'on him'.

As has been said, there are formal 'shlaggin' competitions, culminating in finals, which are high points in Ballykilferret's sporting calendar.

12

The rules of these are complex, and less interesting to the reader than a broad description of the procedure. This is best provided by Gubnet O'Lunacy, who has been taking part in 'shlaggin'' competitions since early boyhood.

'What actually happens, like, is that the men would gather of a summer's evenin', like, outside Gilhooley's pub, or at the creamery gate, like, and maybe they wouldn't have the price of a drink, like. Well, no one would say anything for an hour or so, like. Well, then ye'd know that the shlaggin' would be goin' to start, like, if ye were used to it.

'Well, the lads would get into two cars, or a car and a van, like, and they'd all pile into them and go out to a field somewhere and stand in two lines, like, for the shlaggin' competition.

'Ye must get them all into two cars, like, that's the rule. I've seen twenty or thirty in two cars, and maybe they'd bring a greyhound for good luck, like.

'Well, they'd stand in two lines, like, in the field, and one crowd would be shoutin' "get hup ya boy ya!" and things like that, and the others would shout back, maith an fear or maybe"get up the yard!" like, and they would know that the "shlag" was on them'.

There are many other old games which still thrive in Bally-kilferret in spite of modern commercialised forms of mass entertainment, and whose origins are lost in mist-shrouded antiquity.

One such is the game of 'skelpin'. This might occur when there was a vacuum created by the disappearance of the balls from the pool table in Gilhooley's pub, for instance.

These vanish mysteriously from time to time, and reappear in haycocks, put there as substitutes for hen eggs. Formerly it was the custom to put hen eggs in a man's haycock to bring him bad luck. This was really the placing of a kind of curse or 'pishogue' on the man and his goods. Now the eggs all come in a lorry from the city, so the balls are the nearest substitutes to hand.

The absence of the balls leaves the patrons with nothing to do, and there is generally an adjournment to someone's kitchen, where some youth is usually placed in a chair in the middle of the floor.

The participants in the 'skelpin', all young maidens, sit around the edge of the floor on chairs, and one of them gets an ash plant from the yard, which she keeps behind her back.

It is passed in this manner from person to person until the attention of the central figure is distracted to allow one of the local cailíns to sneak from her chair and give him a 'skelp' on the head with the ash plant.

This procedure continues until every young lady present has succeeded in giving the youth a 'skelp', and the youth is then free to respond in a similar manner to all in the circle. He is rarely able to do this, however, as he is usually lying senseless on the floor by the time his turn comes.

'Skelpin' is believed to have had its origin in the days of landlordism, when the landlord's agent was known as a 'tricky boy' or 'go boy' in the Ballykilferret area. If a family was threatened with eviction by the current agent, the local sages would get together and discuss the matter, and this would be followed by an invitation to the agent for an evening's entertainment in the house of friends of the threatened family.

The evening would begin with a light repast of potatoes for the hosts and the time-honoured plate of ham and tomatoes from the Canon's house for the guest of honour, washed down with copious draughts of a heady liquor, distilled according to a local recipe.

The company would then form a circle around the guest of honour, and the 'skelpin'' would start. The implement used in this instance would be of a very light nature, such as a seagull feather or a sprig of heather, presumably out of deference to the high social standing of the guest.

The game would gather pace throughout the evening, increasing in liveliness and fun with the constant imbibing of the local distillation, until one of the local maidens would dart forward coyly to give her 'skelp', but this time a 'skelp' with a difference! The feather or heather in hand would have been mysteriously replaced by a hatchet!

As the agent lay pouring out his life's blood on the kitchen floor, there would be great joking and the singing of many wild and gay songs, interspersed with ballads telling of the sad history of our country. No one ever thought badly of the

14

hatchet wielder the following day, and her prank was usually described as 'a bit of crack'.

To this day, there is a saying in Ballykilferret when something has been mislaid and cannot be found, that it has 'found an agent's grave'.

THE peculiar ingenuity evidenced in the pastime of 'skelpin' is a characteristic facet of life in Ballykilferret. It is in evidence in the many amateur activities in the town and surrounding districts, such as building, flying and brain surgery.

Let us deal first with building. Many of the people in Ballykilferret suffer from an all-pervading boredom during the long winter months, which is not satisfactorily relieved by such events as rectal music competitions and long-distance spitting contests. The term 'rectal music' demands some explanation, and it is as follows:

The making of rectal music is achieved through compressing bowel wind by use of the sphincter muscle, and then allowing it to escape in a variety of pressures to produce a series of musical notes. Some practitioners of this art have achieved such prowess that they can actually perform whole symphonies, with the most demanding cadenzas.

But to return to the amateur building movement. Many of the local farmers had erected their own pig houses with varying degrees of success, and while discussing the needs of the town one winter's evening, it dawned on Gubnet O'Lunacy that what the town needed was a hotel. This idea was highly praised by all present, and it was decided to build a hotel, using local labour, which would be owned by a co-op. The main attraction of this idea was the healthy grant available from the tourism authorities in the city for this project, and it was felt that no such avenue of finance should remain unexplored by the people of Ballykilferret.

16

The grant was obtained and the hotel was duly constructed with amateur labour, but the remainder of the tale is considered a socially taboo subject in polite society in Ballykilferret. However, this writer feels a conscientious obligation to reveal the facts, since public monies were used in the project.

The day of the grand opening of the hotel dawned greyly, with the odd drop of rain flying in the bitterly cold breeze. It was what one might call an average summer's day; the kind of Irish weather which is such a threat to tourism in countries like Spain and Tunisia.

There were to be solemn speeches and the blessing of the premises by the Canon himself, followed by the traditional meat tea at his house, to be partaken of by only the crème-de-la-crème of Ballykilferret.

The speeches delivered were worthy of Bossuet in full flight, and the party proceeded into the hallway for the solemn blessing by the Canon. He had just begun his impassioned exhortations to the Almighty to look favourably on the building and all who might enjoy its wholesome pleasures, when there was a dull rumbling somewhere deep within the foundations, followed by a cry of, 'Be Jasus lads, I think she's goin' to come down!'

The mass sprint to safety was led by the Canon himself, who surprised all present by displaying such agility for a man of his years, as the building collapsed with the ear-splitting rending of imperfectly finished timber joists and the dull 'crump crump' of heavy slabs of concrete finishing their journey earthwards.

It must also be put on record that allegations were made that not all of the grant had been expended on the hotel, and there may be some truth in these as new pig houses sprang up like mushrooms all over the parish, and certain individuals who had been involved in the building of the hotel had to go to Lourdes to be cured of the ill-effects of the drink which they consumed to calm their shattered nerves.

It was some time before the morale of Ballykilferret recovered from the hotel incident, but with the indomitable optimism which is such an attractive quality in their breed, the people of Ballykilferret embarked, bloody but unbowed, upon the project of starting an amateur flying club.

17

For many years an old light aircraft had been lying out in the haggard of Kilferret Manor, purchased by the present Lord Kilferret's father for the purpose of flying across the Atlantic when such activities were a novelty in distant and more innocent times.

The old Lord Kilferret had lost interest in the project when he discovered that he had been beaten to it by two cads named Alcock and Brown. However, this was probably fortunate, as he had dropped his white stick from the aircraft during a test flight, and the fact that he had mistakenly landed forty miles from Ballykilferret on a racecourse during a point-to-point did not augur well.

Most of the local youths had acquired considerable knowledge of the workings of the internal combustion engine through tinkering with tractors and cars, but this is not to disparage their achievement in bringing the old engine to life again. It was a proud moment for them when it erupted into glorious, roaring fume-laden life.

There was keen interest in the launching, and the excited crowds watched the intrepid local flier lift off over the trees. Their admiration for him was heightened by the knowledge that it was his first time at the controls of an aircraft. Such a splendid achievement!

When it became apparent after some hours that the aircraft was not going to return, search parties were sent out, but no trace of it or its heroic pilot was ever found.

The loss of the aircraft was considered a great tragedy, not so much because of the disappearance of the young flier, but because various local youths had invested sums as large as two pounds a man in its refurbishment. These mercenary people even went as far as to suggest that the gallant youth had stolen the aircraft and was hiding out somewhere, in Manchester or Birmingham, say, waiting for the furore to die down.

To this day they have been steaming open his mother's post in the hope that he will try to communicate with her, but so far, I am glad to relate, they have been disappointed.

The amateur brain surgery movement was a little more successful, although it might be argued that the mere survival of the patient is not an adequate criterion of success

18

in such a delicate skill.

The only visible trace of the experiments in brain surgery in Ballykilferret is the tendency of certain individuals to walk around in ever-decreasing circles until they slump to the ground in a dizzy, puzzled state, but they soon recover from these attacks and continue on their way as though nothing had happened.

An end was put to the brain surgery activities in Ballykilferret by the Gardaí, after a local maiden of hitherto mild disposition, mounted a bicycle and rode at breakneck speed down the hallway of the Garda Station, causing considerable damage and injury in the day room.

The account of the aforegoing happenings was passed between the philosophers and wits of Ballykilferret to the accompaniment of sniggers and sharp little pucks in the ribs, which are known as 'puckin'.

One might be tempted to think that the practice of nudging one's neighbour in the ribs is the same the world over, but this is not so in the case of Ballykilferret.

There exists a strange convention in Ballykilferret whereby statements and questions are accompanied by what, to the uninitiated, would appear to be particularly savage attacks with the balled fist to the rib cage and abdomen. To add to the apparent viciousness of these, the assailant contrives to have one knuckle protruding from the fist, karate-style, to ensure the greatest possible discomfort to the recipient of the 'puck'.

The 'puck' generally produces no discernible effect other than a faint flicker in the grimly smiling eyes of the recipient, but in exceptional cases there is a glazing of the eyes and the victim is felled to the ground. The victor never acknowledges his win, but goes on his way as though nothing has happened. It is up to the loser then to find an opportunity for revenge.

There have been cases of Ballykilferret people waiting for up to three years for the opportunity to return a 'puck'. It is to be noted that any overt response to a 'puck', such as the disappearance of the smile, which should always remain, or a faint stagger, is considered a serious loss of face.

A typical scene would be that of two men meeting in the

19

main street of Ballykilferret, one home from England for Christmas. The returned emigrant would ask: 'Well, Mick, how's it goin'?' and this would be accompanied by a well-timed 'puck', causing the smiling victim to turn bright green in the face.

A year might elapse and the bold emigrant might be home for the Christmas, having forgotten the encounter of the previous year and ready to impress the simple local folk with his fine new clothes and urban gait. His first promenade would be brutally cut short with, 'Well, Seán, how are they all in England?' and a searing jab to the soft part under the ribs which would cause him to slump to his knees, retching.

Nobody knows when the custom of 'puckin' began in Ballykilferret, but it has had no small effect on the fortunes of the town, and the surrounding townlands.

THE sycophancy of hundreds of years did not go unnoticed by the British Crown, and contemplating the forthcoming celebrations to mark her Golden Jubilee, the late Queen Victoria was studying the map of her enormous Empire with some intensity, deciding what honours should go to what parts, according to their varying degrees of loyalty.

One obscure parish in Ireland came high on the list, to the surprise of Her Majesty and her advisers. British influence had reached most parts of the world, and had governed with relative stability in many for long periods, but nowhere on that red-flecked map was there a place with such an unbroken record of unswerving complicity with the British Crown in 'subduing the natives'.

The odd assegai had been thrown on the Dark Continent from time to time. Throats were cut and maidens ravished in the border areas of India every now and then, but the record of loyalty in Ballykilferret was without stain of any colour.

'This must be acknowledged', screamed the old queen, veteran of a thousand intrigues of state, on whose chessboard of human misery the sun never set. So great was her agitation that she rose from Her bath water, capsizing many models of the British Fleet in the process and sending the Lords of the Admiralty scurrying from the room, prepared to face death rather than such an awe-inspiring sight again.

It was tactfully pointed out to her majesty that a state visit to Ballykilferret might result in some embarrassment to the Government, since not all parts of Ireland had shown such unswerving loyalty as this parish, but her majesty was adamant. 'I don't care how the hell yez do it', she croaked, the adrenalin coursing through her old veins afresh, 'but if yez don't, we will go berserk!'

21

Thus it came to pass that a warship of her majesty's fleet anchored far out in Dublin Bay, ostensibly 'on exercises', and a small craft put out from her, rowed by two jack-tars, with a heavily shawled, but somewhat regal figure seated in the stern, and headed through a choppy sea for Kingstown.

The inhabitants of Ballykilferret were ecstatic at the prospect of her majesty's visit, although it was to be somewhat subdued in tone. This was to be the crowning moment in a relationship which had been built up over hundreds of years, and which had sent many a 'rebel villain' to the rack and the gallows.

The organisers of the civic reception of her majesty's honour had spared no ingenuity in the arrangements for her delectation. There was to be a series of gala events throughout the day, culminating in a mouth-watering meat tea at the then canon's house. There were excesses it is true, but this is to be expected in a simple community which is suddenly faced with the responsibility of playing host to an empress, and their very naïveté lent them a certain charm.

This charm was not acknowledged by the bishop, who afterwards disciplined the canon for concelebrating a service with the local Church of Ireland clergyman in the private chapel of Ballykilferret Manor, to the accompaniment of céilí dancing by the Act of Union Dancers, and a military two-step, performed by the local British officers and their wives.

Most of the festivities went off without a hitch throughout the day, and Her Majesty had just completed Her speech of praise to the people of Ballykilferret, when one, O Lubhnasa Chluais Chapall, or 'O'Lunacy of the Horse's Ears' so called for his ability to hear seditious conversations at a great range and report them to the authorities, sidled forward towards her Majesty on the dais raised for the occasion, grinning widely from ear to ear, and looking as though he was about to say something of import.

O'Lunacy was the 'big wheel' of the town at the time, and Her Majesty had been judiciously informed of this. Thus it was that she inclined Her head to him in an attitude of listening, and this was Her undoing. Had she remained erect, at least Her diaphragmatic muscles would have been better

22

positioned to withstand what followed, but how was She to know?'

O'Lunacy reached the Royal Personage, and no one actually saw the 'puck' as it sped to its mark. Victoria, Queen of the United Kingdom of Great Britain and Ireland, Empress of India, only child of Edward, Duke of Kent (fourth son of George III) and Victoria Maria Louisa (sister of King Leopold of the Belgians), slid to the ground with a thin sibilant expulsion of breath.

The meat tea at the Canon's house went untasted, and the flow of payments for information received dwindled to a negligible trickle, marking the beginning of Ballykilferret's economic downward slide.

WHEN the amateur brain surgery came to an end, it was felt that pressure was being put on the Garda Sergeant by the professionals of the town, particularly one Myles Grannerty, merchant prince, whose many interests include ownership of Grannerty's Supermarket, which might be described as the true hub of Ballykilferret's commercial life.

Mr Grannerty is included among such obvious examples of professionalism as the Canon and the local doctor, Dr O'Trembler, not because the writer would dare to equate mere lowly commerce with the rarified aura of those who have 'got a degree above in the city', but because of his unique sensitivity and skill in the use of the bacon slicer, which he has honed lovingly to produce an expertise which can only be described as pure art.

Mr Grannerty's renown as a performer is so great that it has successfully overidden a couple of major blows to his public image. It is to the credit of his admirers that they can divorce in their minds the ridicule which followed these setbacks to an otherwise unblemished career from their acknowledgement of his undoubted artistic prowess.

Like all great artists, Mr Grannerty does not suffer fools gladly. This does not make him the easiest person in the world to live with, so maybe it is not unreasonable to expect that he might make some enemies during the course of his distinguished career.

Such was the case with the adolescent 'Lunar' Murphy who served an apprenticeship in Mr Grannerty's shop. He acquired this appellation at the time when the first pictures of the lunar landscape were being published on the local newspaper, *The Ballykilferret Bugle*.

The similarity between the lunar landscape and the fiery, suppurating acne of Lunar's neck and cheeks was remarked by a local wit and philosopher, and in the cruel tradition of small communities the name remained, and will remain until poor Lunar's bones fertilize the soil of Ballykilferret for generations who will never know him.

Mr Grannerty not being an easy task-master, Lunar's apprenticeship was no bed of roses. Most of the heavy hauling and pulling of supplies for the shop was done by Lunar. He was often seen to stagger from a lorry outside the shop with an enormous bag of meal on his head, and so great would be his exertion that the unfortunate youth's acne would suppurate visibly with each grunt of breath. To add to his torments, it was not unusual for a small boy to stick out his foot in front of poor Lunar, who would travel forward with greatly increased speed into the shop, carrying all before him.

On one memorable occasion he travelled straight through the hardware department, demolishing eighteen dinner services in his path before exiting through a window at the back of the store which was closed at the time, and ending up head-first in the water butt at the rear.

Mr Grannerty, attracted by the commotion, rushed into the yard to be scandalised by shouts of 'Yez shower of shites, and yer mothers before yez!' as Lunar emerged dripping from the water butt. As Mr Grannerty pointed out, before deducting a small fine from Lunar's meagre pay packet, 'We can't have the customers listening to filth the likes of that from filth the likes of you!'

This unfortunate incident was followed by what looked

25

like an uneasy truce between Lunar and Mr Grannerty until 'Sausage Day' came. 'Sausage Day' in Ballykilferret is the day when the lorry arrives from the city with supplies of fresh sausages aboard, and there is a veritable stampede by housewives to purchase the coveted succulent sausages for which Mr Grannerty's emporium is renowned.

The women were four-deep at the counter, and Mr Grannerty was wrapping orders with his usual air of disdain, when the brooding Lunar took the opportunity to steal from the shop, bent on a peculiarly inventive revenge upon his employer.

He moved down the street with his strange rapid bobbing gait, the product of years of carrying heavy sacks, and turned into what is known locally as 'Sweetie Miller's Lane'.

This lane derives its name from its sole inhabitant, who affects certain strange characteristics, such as carrying a handbag occasionally, and wearing a toupee of a challenging shade of red. In the handbag he carries supplies of sweets which he distributes to the altarboys on their way home from Benediction. At the appearance of the Canon on the horizon, he suddenly scuttles down his lane, blushing furiously, and because of this he has the reputation locally of being 'shy in himself'.

Lunar made his way down the lane and paused to root in the long grass which skirted it, and from it he withdrew a large tomcat which had apparently been in collision with a tractor, with somewhat unpleasant results. To add to this the dead animal had lain for some days in the lane.

The acne-tortured youth carried the cat carefully, and with an air of great purpose, up the lane and back up the main street towards Mr Grannerty's shop.

In the shop Mr Grannerty was exercising his natural authority over the ladies with the severity for which he is renowned.

'Get back in the queue there, or yez'll get no bloody sausages at all', he cried, with the assurance which comes from knowing that you have a near-monopoly of trade. The ladies were suitably subdued, and Mr Grannerty continued to wrap purchases with agonising deliberation.

He didn't see his apprentice enter the shop, and was in the

middle of wrapping an order with particular panache, when he heard a voice say, 'There's a sample, Mr Grannerty. I'll have the others up to ye later. They makes great sausages!' and he felt a heavy thump on his chest as the dead and festering tomcat stuck him and fell to the counter.

The ladies vanished from the shop like water through a sieve, leaving Mr Grannerty entirely alone, as Lunar had preceded the ladies after delivering his momentous oration and hurling the cat. Mr Grannerty had the appearance of a man who has suddenly been pumped full of cold porridge. It was some time before the sausage trade revived in Grannerty's Supermarket.

Another time when Mr Grannerty lost face publicly was when things went wrong with the dinner party given by the Bank Manager's Wife. The unfortunate thing about this incident was that, although Mr Grannerty was publicly exonerated in the matter, his dignity suffered through his mere involvement.

One day Mr Grannerty was lovingly stacking small packets of cooking lard in ornate patterns on his shelves to while away a slack period, when his reveries were rudely interrupted by the socially-conscious tones of the Bank Manager's Wife, demanding a dozen fillet steaks, some fish for a fish course, and some rather exotic French cheeses.

Mr Grannerty, being accustomed to doling out the more humble fare of tins of beans and boxes of processed cheese, suffered severe pulmonary embarrassment on hearing the order of the Bank Manager's Wife, so much so that he had to lean for a short time on the counter to regain his breath.

Unfortunately, the leaning attitude and the panting produced a somewhat fixed expression in the eyes, which the Bank Manager's Wife interpreted as total incomprehension. She began her order again in considerably raised tones, only to be reminded by Mr Grannerty that there was nothing wrong with his hearing, and he would have lost a valuable customer but for the near-monopoly-of-trade situation.

The day of the dinner party dawned, and there was much careful preparation of the food, which had been procured with considerable difficulty by Mr Grannerty.

Shortly before the guests were due to arrive, young Nuala,

the hired help from the town, entered the kitchen to find the cat with its nose to the fish course in the mistaken belief that all its birthdays had come at once. The cat was duly grabbed by Nuala and ejected from the kitchen into the garden without ceremony. The guests arrived and dinner commenced.

The guests were taking leave of their hostess after what had been a very successful evening, standing about the doorstep in the fine night and indulging in the sort of chit-chat which generally acompanies such leave-takings, when to their horror, they found the body of the Bank Manager's cat deep in rigor mortis on the grass margin. The situation was complicated by the arrival of young Nuala at the door to announce that she had seen the cat at the fish earlier in the evening.

The unfortunate guests were galvanised into action. Some took to the shrubbery, where they forced their fingers down their throats in an effort to retrieve the offending toxic substance from their systems; others leapt into their cars and drove fast for the county hospital and the stomach pump, and the remainder became hysterical, running around in circles wringing their hands and imagining the onset of all sorts of horrible symptoms.

The news of what had happened spread through the town by mid-morning the next day, having been sped on its way by young Nuala, who issued a press release in the Alcatraz Bar Grill and Chip Shop on the way home from the party, and aided by bulletins from folk in the town who had contacts on the staff of the county hospital.

It was known throughout the entire area that the food for the dinner party had been purchased at Grannerty's Supermarket, and Mr Grannerty, knowing this, was mortified. The day passed with the town in a ferment of speculation about the cause of the contamination.

Was it true that Mr Grannerty owed a considerable sum of money to the bank as a result of a private arrangement between himself the Bank Manager, and his attempt to liquidate the Bank manager, his wife and the debt in one fell swoop had failed?

Could it be that Lunar still harboured his ancient grudge against Mr Grannerty, and in an insane desire to compromise Mr Grannerty, had risked the lives of several others? Visions of Mr Grannerty being led handcuffed to the Garda car with a blanket thrown over his head to save him from the prying lens of the one camera of *The Ballykilferret Bugle* loomed large in the minds of all those who had ever been made to feel inferior by Mr Grannerty.

On the second day after the fateful party, the bank manager's wife answered the chimes of her hall door, which rang through the house with the haunting call of an ice cream van. On the doorstep stood her neighbour, embarrassed and shame-faced.

'I don't know how you'll ever forgive us', she squawked in tones not dissimilar to those used by the bank manager's Wife herself when climbing socially, 'but Liam and I hit your cat with the car when we were coming in the other night from the golf club, and it must have made off in the dark because we couldn't find it when we got out of the car. We didn't like to tell you because we knew you had company in, and we were away in the city all day yesterday'.

MR Grannerty's skill with the bacon slicer
has given rise to an activity peculiar to the area of Ballykilferret, which is preceded by a ritual akin to the mysterious
assembly of the swallows prior to migration.

Bidden by some mysterious rallying force, they gather for
this great event, and in much the same way the youths of
Ballykilferret foregather around the door of the local pub,
Gilhooley's, prior to going to watch the bacon slicer. No
one has ever been able to divine the instinctive magnetism
which brings about this gathering but it has been noted that
it is generally accompanied by the weekly cycle of impecun-
ity which occurs on the day prior to payment of unemploy-
ment assistance.

Nothing is said for some hours as the crowd of youths
swells around the door of the pub, and nothing is to be heard
save the utterance of the odd expletive, such as 'ah bollocks'

and the 'phut' sound of the occasional stream of saliva as it begins its sad flight to extinction in the dust. Then suddenly, as though bidden by the spirit at a prayer meeting, one of the youths will say, 'I'm gettin' ten fags and goin' down to Grannerty's to watch the bacon slicer'.

No contrary desire is ever expressed, and the speaker is followed by a silent line of youths, their hands thrust deep in their pockets, their eyes fixed upon the ground as they kick angrily at discarded cigarette packets and chewing-gum wrappers, headed for the unimaginable delights of watching Mr Grannerty operate the bacon slicer in his small supermarket with the skill and lofty finesse of the true master.

Mr Grannerty is aware of their approach towards his shop, although no one would expect such a masterly exponent of his craft to acknowledge this.

To the casual observer, the only indication that Mr Grannerty is anticipating the lonely calvary of his art would be his deft selection of an extra-large piece of choice ham from the shelf under the counter, and its placing upon the prongs of the gleaming slicer.

As in the case of all great artists, the apparent ease with which these actions are executed is the fruit of long and gruelling practice.

He does not acknowledge his audience at first as they sidle around the door of the shop and seat themselves furtively on the row of orange crates under the window, their labels tempting the mind to dream of hot sunny climes.

The afternoon sun streams through the window, the cigarette smoke swirling lazily through the silver motes in its beam, and just as its searching rays glint upon the gleaming majesty of the bacon slicer, the shuttle goes into its beautiful hypnotic rythmic action and the delicious pink slices fall with balletic grace from the blade on the piece of grease-proof paper placed beneath with such loving artistic skill.

The tension mounts as the pile of pink slices grows. For what jaded palate are they destined? Is the Canon's mysterious wealthy sister in town with her fur coat and white shoes for yet another of his housekeeper's meat teas? Has her ladyship up at the Manor House had another of her turns, and is his lordship having to fend for himself again in the kitchen? Etiquette would forbid any direct enquiry, but still the imagination is tickled.

Now Mr Grannerty is coming to the end of the piece of bacon, and various small coins begin to make their appearance among the still silent watchers. Unspoken, the bets are laid as to how many slices Mr Grannerty will manage to make of the remaining heel of ham. Suddenly the air is rent with cries of: 'He'll not get the dozen! He'll not get the dozen this night!' and: 'Begod he will. I never seen him bet yet. Me life on ye Mr G. oul' stock!'

Just as the tension is becoming unbearable, Mr Grannerty, with the certainty of the truly great performer that his audience is completely at his mercy, lifts his hand slowly from the turning handle of the slicer, and with great deliberation reaches up to remove the sodden brown, and still burning cigarette butt from one side of his mouth where it is in danger of branding the lip.

He places it carefully in the other side, then pushes his cracked spectacles up the bridge of his nose to relieve the irritation caused by the sweat of his artistic tour-de-force, and rummages briefly in one hairy nostril before he places his large hand once again upon the turning handle. The cigarette ash falls eloquently like a grey worm on the slices of ham below.

This is the climax, the long-awaited moment of perfection, no different from the anticipation by a sultan of the completion of the houris' dance. There is a thin sussuration from the cruel blade; the slice falls, and there are cries of: 'Jasus, did ye ever see the beatin' of him!' 'He never lost it, and how would he? Sure wasn't it in the family?' 'Well of course he has the wrists for it. D'ye see, it's in the hands!'

This release of tension is followed by a general exodus of the audience from the shop into the lane beside. Cigarettes are lit, and as the bright streams of yellow, long-held urine converge on the muddy ground, the bets are laid for a further great artistic spectacle as Mr Grannerty reaches beneath his cornucopian counter for yet another piece of ham.

THE name of Dr O'Trembler has been mentioned as a member of the alleged pressure group to put an end to Ballykilferret's amateur brain surgery, but even if his professional interests had not been affected, his name as an objector would have been an obvious choice by those who harbour resentments as a result of collision with his crabbed personality.

This results from an extreme sense of inferiority stemming from the background of a small hill farm. One might well ask what there is to be ashamed of in a farming background, but then it is to be remembered that snobs are born, not made. Indeed, it is to the eternal credit of the late parents of Dr

O'Trembler that they spawned three lady national school teachers and one doctor in their stony lot. A few miserable wind-blown sheep and a thatched mud cabin would hardly seem to be suitable inspiration for such academic achievements, but one must not reckon without the mysterious indomitable ambitions of man.

It was the combined contributions from the three salaries of his sisters that purchased Dr O'Trembler the first two pairs of underpants he had ever owned when he went to the city to study medicine, and it was those three salaries which kept him in the style to which he was unaccustomed while his sense of shame about his background festered.

His feeling of inferiority was not diminished by the knowledge that his father had told everyone he could lay hands on in Ballykilferret that his son had 'gone on for the doctorin' because he hadn't the brains for the sheep farmin'.

Having imparted this gratuitous gem, the O'Trembler senior would bury his indescribably dirty claw deeper into his captive's shoulder and lapse into helpless giggles as he envoloped him in a breath-constricting cloud of halitosis.

Dr O'Trembler encountered several examination setbacks in the course of his studies, and his chances of practising professionally were finally salvaged by an anachronistic body of apothecaries whose power to grant licences was withdrawn shortly after Dr O'Trembler had the good fortune to slip under the net.

It may not be mere coincidence that, to this day, the mere mention of the word 'leeches' causes Dr O'Trembler to bring about a rapid change in the subject of conversation.

Another cause of Dr O'Trembler's somewhat abrasive disposition might be that he is self-conscious about his gait, which is slightly impaired owing to an unfortunate injury to the *glutimus maximus,* sustained in the course of his professional duties.

This occurred while he was dealing with a particularly hysterical child who had to be given an injection. The child, a small boy of some three years, was protesting volubly and violently that the injection was unnecessary, and Dr O'Trembler admonished the mother to take no nonsense from him.

Between them they held him down, and the treatment was

administered, despite the unremitting squeals and wriggles of the patient.

Dr O'Trembler was washing his hands at the basin in the surgery with his back turned disdainfully towards the child, and the mother was gazing through the window, recovering from the ordeal of witnessing her beloved offspring's agony, and listening to the good doctor's somewhat pompous discourse on the subject of child rearing.

The doctor affected a clipped, military style of speech, which he felt gave him an air of authority when dealing with his rustic patients.

'Take no nonsense from 'em, 'at's what I say. A little discipline never did a child any harm. Treat 'em army-style, 'at's what I say. Children are too damned spoiled nowadays, 'at's what I say. Give 'em jankers now and then, 'at's what I say'.

Neither the doctor nor the mother saw the child as he crept stealthily forwards, bent on revenge. Indeed, the first inkling they had that he had actually left the couch was when he rammed the empty syringe into the Doctor's bottom with a cry of, 'bold doctor not do that again!'

The doctor has subsequently developed a distinctive style of furtive, stiff-legged scuttling as he leaves his car to enter the homes of patients on his house calls.

THE undisputed leader of the professional élite in Ballykilferret is the Canon, who fulfils his onerous role with an unswerving bleak dignity; the sort of patrician aura which must have surrounded the great aristocratic Papal aspirants of the middle ages, groomed for high office from the cradle.

Thus, his housekeeper has that air of mystery and responsibility about her which surrounds the good sisters who attend to the intimate personal everyday needs of His Holiness the Pope.

The Canon's father was a retired ballroom owner and gaming machine proprietor, who had hurriedly sold up his business interests and run to rural anonymity with what remained of his capital, his creditors snapping savagely at his heels. He purchased what had formerly been a small coaching hotel, and married a shy, retiring girl, settling down to enjoy what promised to be a golden decade or so of freedom from mysterious persons leaping at him from dark corners and attempting to break his legs and arms, or cut his face with razors.

His dreams were never to be fulfilled, however. The shy retiring girl showed a remarkable aptitude for the business, and soon blossomed into a tough, obese and garrulous hostess, who quickly built up a highly profitable bar trade, to the complete exclusion of the hotel side of things.

The hostlery soon attracted the flashy travelling salesman type of the day and a host of tipsters and gentlemen who, although they had no visible means of support, were said to be 'in business', and had unlimited funds to spend on drink.

It was said by some uncharitable people that the establishment was staffed with the illegitimate offspring of these gentlemen, but then success in business will always create a counter-wave of jealousy.

The fact is, though, that the source of supply of these young people always remained a mystery. They were of stunted growth, boys and girls alike, and although their outward appearance held little promise of keenness of intellect, they exhibited an uncanny facility with figures while serving drinks, which accelerated in achievement as the hours wore on towards breakfast time.

One twelve-year-old-boy was seen by some of the clientèle at a midland race meeting, emerging from the bar wiping his mouth and smelling strongly of whiskey, complete with camel-hair coat and enormous racing binoculars. On being hailed, he sidled over to them and imparted a couple of tips from the corner of his mouth, which proved to be highly profitable, before striding with the air of a man of destiny towards a bookmaker's stand.

Later that evening they were surprised to find him going serenely about his tasks in the 'hotel'. How had he travelled the long distance in the time, to be there so long before them?

'Ah, sure I just took an oul' taxi the sixty miles, 'cause Her Ladyship would send me away to where I came from if I was late back' was the reply.

No doubt it was this sort of statement which caused un-

37

charitable speculation as to the source of the 'hotel's' labour supply.

Because of the late hours of the trade, the Canon's mother slept late each day, rising around noon to eat a gargantuan breakfast, served by a gnome-like youth, who was once described by a customer as being 'only up from the Aran Islands three days, not a word of English to him, and has us all by the privates'.

This great lady would then settle down to read the racing pages of the newspaper and the stock exchange trends in detail, before she finally exchanged her florid dressing gown, (which did little to hide a cleavage which merited mention in the *Guinness Book of Records*), for the creation of the day.

As can be readily seen, there was but little time left in her life to devote to her husband, and it was in one of these precious moments that the Canon was conceived. The pleasure of the encounter was somewhat marred for the Canon's father, however, by the fact that his wife called him by the name of a particularly flashy salesman who frequented the bar, before she rose hurriedly from the bed saying 'Lord God, I must be out of me senses altogether takin' chances like this', and rushed from the room to attend to her duties as hostess.

It was into this atmosphere inimical to proper family life that the Canon was born, and he was soon sent to be minded by a maiden aunt until he could walk about, because his mother decided, quite rightly, that a busy 'hotel' was 'no fit place for an infant'.

So busy was she kept with the 'hotel', that the Canon's mother was quite unaware of the decline in her husband's health, or the fact that he had aged so rapidly since marrying her, and it was with some surprise that she learned of his death from the aforementioned gnome, who told her: 'I think himself is after goin' to his Maker earlier this evenin', but I didn't like to tell ye when ye were busy with the customers'.

The Canon's childhood was spent in the nether regions of the premises under the feet of the scurrying staff, and it was this existence which armed him with his first few phrases, which consisted of 'under me shaggin' feet all day, ye little snot ye', and 'root in the arse if I trip over ye again'.

It was a wise decision of his mother's which sent the Canon far from such coarsening influences to the care of the Jesuits, whence he returned briefly before being despatched for 'holidays' to the maiden aunt, or a succession of summer courses at Irish language colleges.

The boy found refuge from his loneliness in his studies, and his progress through the seminary was marked by high academic honours. After ordination, his fleeting visits home to the 'hotel' brought about severe curtailment in the late serving of drinks, and it was with a sense of relief that he returned to his pastoral duties from an atmosphere of sudden pauses in conversation and hasty changes of subject.

Although his mother was, indeed, extremely proud of her son's high calling, she once succumbed sufficiently to the exasperation caused by his visits to remark to a customer: 'The Lord bless us and preserve us, and may His Holy Mother look down on us, but ye wouldn't turn a bloody shillin' with a priesteen in the house!'

Late in life, the poor woman suffered a severe stroke, and it is to her eternal credit that she had amassed a fund of goodwill during her business career sufficient to provide her with the voluntary services of the womenfolk of former patrons to minister to and manipulate her immense bulk in shifts around the clock, keeping her constantly supplied with sips of warm brandy.

Towards the end, in a moment of lucidity, she expressed a desire to have Mass said in her room, and the Canon was duly summoned to perform the ceremony.

His mother maintained her lucid state, to the satisfaction of her nurses, throughout the first part of the Mass, propped high on lace-edged pillows with a beatific expression on her face and the remains of a glass of warm brandy clutched underneath the bedclothes, but at the elevation of the chalice by her son, she rose to a sitting position, to the horror of the assembly, and raised her brandy glass on high with a cry of 'Cheers son! I never thought ye'd get round to takin' a sup. Sláinte go saol!' She fell back upon the pillows, comatose, in which state she remained until her death.

39

SOME of the more up-to-date community activities have found their way to Ballykilferret, such as the breeding of rats for racing by the Ballykilferret Rat Breeder's Club, and of course the I.C.A., which brings country-women together for so many worthwhile purposes. The I.C.A. is a relative newcomer to Ballykilferret, and its progress has suffered only one small setback to date.

The fateful chain of events which led to this setback began with the arrival of one Filbert O'Lunacy to the farm of his uncle Norbert, cousin to the famed Gubnet, for the weekend from the city.

As is the wont of idle visitors to farms, Filbert was wandering around the yard watching the work of his uncle, Maolruin, brother of Norbert, doing various tasks of husbandry.

It is always a pleasure to watch others work, but it can be particularly annoying to feel curious eyes upon you while you go about your tasks. Such was the feeling of Maolruin, as he squirmed under the gaze of his nephew.

The reader might protest that all work has an intrinsic

dignity, and that surely there was no valid reason for Maolruin to squirm, but it must be explained that Maolruin has never enjoyed the independence of spirit and the fulfilment which goes with self-employment.

He is what is described as a 'second son', and thus the farm went to his elder brother, Norbert, on the death of their father. He was left without inheritance or employment, and completely at the tender mercy of his brother.

Perhaps he would not have taken the job offered to him if he had heard Norbert mutter: 'Be japers I have ye now, ye shite!' as he walked from the kitchen after the reading of their father's will, but since that time he has been subjected to the most excruciating indignities by his brother.

He has worked long hours at the most menial tasks in return for a hard bed in an outhouse and a meagre diet of scraps, and this experience has seriously affected his self-confidence and personal development.

The knowledge that Filbert O'Lunacy had escaped from the spiritually-confining atmosphere of Ballykilferret to the sophistication and freedom of the city, with its lurid delights, did nothing to diminish Maolruin's sense of inferiority.

'Young fellas has the divil an' all of a time nowadays', he thought as he straightened up from his back-breaking labours, his eyes travelling from the toes of Filbert's shiny cowboy boots by way of his new jeans to his floral shirt and pendant.

He couldn't bring himself to meet the confident and superior gaze which beamed laser-like from under the lustrous barbered black thatch. He felt as though he was being studied with clinical detachment by a beautiful lady anthropologist.

Had he but spent a few days as a co-dishwasher of Filbert in the Greasy Spoon Cafe, Maolruin would have taken solace from the knowledge that Filbert was not considered an intellectual colossus by his fellow workers in that steaming den of creativity, but his confinement in Ballykilferret has bred in Maolruin incurable fantasies about city life, of the ceaseless thump of dance music, and an endless vista of steaming bags of freshly-cooked chips.

Anyone who could cope with such a lifestyle has achieved

dizzying heights of sophistication in Maolruin's eyes.

Such a person would never have to demean himself by performing the task which now faced Maolruin: ringing the sow. The job of placing the rings in the beast's snout was difficult enough in itself, without having the undignified postures imposed upon one by her antics witnessed by this urban masher.

Maolruin's eyes remained at pendant level, and a faintly derisory smile flickered at the corners of his mouth, undisturbed by the act of speech which was performed between firmly clenched teeth, to the accompaniment of rapid inhalations and exhalations of breath.

'I suppose ye'd have no heart for ringin' a sow now that ye're a city slicker with yer fine job above?'

Filbert's protestations of democracy and willingness to help were met with a scornful shake of the head and toss of the shoulders from Maolruin, and it was not without an element of bravado that Maolruin performed the difficult task of throwing his arthritic leg over the wall of the pigsty and following it with the other one in a half-vaulting action.

It is said of certain animals such as dolphins and baboons that they possess a marked degree of intelligence, but such researches will not be complete until they include an exhaustive study of the female swine.

A keen observer would have been aware of the sow's intense study of the two men during their conversation, and the almost hominoid manner in which she appeared to comprehend their words. Her red-eyed gaze had the unwavering, suspicious and resentful quality which is to be seen in the scrutiny which comes from under the shawls of ancient desert crones.

Had Filbert not been away for some time from farm life, with its natural rhythms and reflexes, he might not have performed the next act in this drama, but perform it he did by opening the bolt to the door of the pigsty enclosure just as Maolruin lost his balance in the slippery mud after his cavalier crossing of the wall.

He stumbled forward and was forced to place a leg across the animal's back owing to the cramped conditions of the enclosure, just as she seized the opportunity to crash through

42

the open door with the speed of an express train.

In retrospect, the sight of Maolruin astride the sow's back going across the yard at such an alarming speed is not without its amusing aspect, but it must be remembered that Maolruin's alarm was further increased by the knowledge that the sow was rapidly running out of space to pursue her mad course. Soon she must halt or collide with the kitchen door, causing serious injury to herself and her rider.

But providence was to deal a chance of survival to Maolruin. The kitchen door was unlatched and merely pulled to, enabling the demented animal to thunder through the room, to the consternation of Mrs O'Lunacy, Maolruin's sister-in-law, who was performing the delicate task of removing the film from her camera under a dish cloth to keep it from the light.

It was said of Mrs O'Lunacy when she was still a young girl that she was 'a fine comfortable woman with her arse close to the ground, that'd throw ye a child once a year'. It was also said of her that she had 'legs on her that'd kick-start a jumbo jet'.

The reader may gather from these descriptions that she was considered a girl of ample proportions, but he will have a clearer idea of her present dimensions if he tries to imagine the effects of twenty years of exclusively starchy food and ten hours' sleep a night with 'a little rest on in the mornings' until lunch time. Add to this an insatiable passion for chocolate and sweets and you have a woman who has been described locally as a person who 'must have to get her knickers on prescription'.

Maolruin still attributes the remarkable escape of himself and the sow from serious injury to the amplitude of the region covered by the said knickers, but this is small consolation to Mrs O'Lunacy, who had to explain to her I.C.A. colleagues how the only pictures of their annual outing were ruined by being exposed to the light.

The knickers, however, were replaceable. Because of their enormous size they have to be specially ordered from the city, and the reserve supply rests in a large cardboard box on the shelves of the local general draper's, along with many cards of strong knicker elastic in case of breakdowns.

Iᴛ is interesting to note that the problem of alcoholism is unknown in Ballykilferret. There are, of course, those who 'take a drink'. True, it might be said that they take this drink at very frequent intervals throughout the day. One might even say that eight o'clock in the morning is too early to start, but surprisingly there are no alcoholics in Ballykilferret. The nearest thing to an alcoholic in Ballykilferret is what might be described as the 'heavy drinker'.

Ballykilferret is light years ahead of the most up-to-date welfare state in the world in its approach to heavy drinking. It has evolved a means of helping the heavy drinker which shows an unmatched sociological compassion.

No one knows quite how the scheme is funded. It may be that the manager of the labour exchange has the ear of the relevant government minister, or more likely he has found some discretionary way of diverting funds at his disposal towards the tangible benefit of the citizens, but he has devised the 'Heavy Drinker's Allowance', which will no doubt be copied by social architects all over the globe.

This operates as follows: The heavy drinker receives a book of green coupons from the manager at the local labour exchange who exercises a discretion in the issuing of these books. Each coupon can be exchanged at the local public house for one pint of stout, and in exceptional cases the applicant is issued with a book of red coupons, which he can exchange for balls of malt.

'Aha', I hear the reader cry, 'but what happens if the weather is too bad for the drinker to go to the pub? What happens if he is locked in by the rainy season?'

The answer is simple. The drinker merely saves his coupons during the bad weather, and he may exchange them with the manager for what is known locally as 'dry money'. Surely it is hard to imagine a more enlightened approach to social welfare?

The stentorian tones of Mr Grannerty when dealing with unruly housewives are matched only by those of Mr Gilhooley when announcing closing time in his bar. This admirable vocal ability has been developed by long years of exercise, caused by the inexplicable reluctance in Ballykilferret to depart from the premises when there is no further possibility of obtaining liquor.

Mr Gilhooley has devised a range of ingenious methods of clearing his bar, which should be of interest to the student of local customs. As he explains it himself:

'Ye can tell by their eyes, like. Some nights they'd be talkin' away, and ye'd see a kind of glazed look comin' on them, and ye'd know by the look of them what ye'd have to do to get them out, like. Ye'd know that all the shoutin' in the world wouldn't shift them'.

One means he employs is to smash a heavy ash tray to pieces on the counter, scattering the sharp fragments into the faces of the customers. But there are many nights when this has no visible effect on them, and the conversation continues as though nothing has occurred.

45

It is then that Mr Gilhooley might resort to the tactic of singling out the leader of the conversation and telling him news of some alarming domestic tragedy, such as a bereavement or the collapse of a roof. But it is not uncommon for the recipient of this news to continue his discourse, untroubled by the shock bulletin and apparently unaware that Mr Gilhooley has spoken to him.

News of an impending bereavement is most likely to produce a reaction when there is some advantage to be gained through the death. An example of this occurred recently, when the hearer, being falsely informed of the imminent death of his brother, rushed home to check the authenticity of the news, not out of concern for the welfare of the brother, but because there was a dispute over grazing rights between the two men.

Mr Gilhooley has even gone to the lengths of firing blasts from a shotgun through the ceiling, but this generally goes unacknowledged unless some minor injury is caused, such as an instance when one of the customers lost a piece of his ear.

When he complained about this to Mr Gilhooley he had to accept the logic of the argument that he should consider himself lucky to have received such a minor injury, as he 'might have lost the whole head'.

Mr Gilhooley has one unfailing means of emptying his premises which he only uses with great reluctance and as a last resort. This consists in unleashing his three savage alsations upon the customers, but he finds this distasteful as it tends to upset these sensitive animals, and they risk injury from the retaliatory boots of the clientèle.

One persevering patron was driven from the premises by the dogs, leaving behind him a half-finished pint of stout, and re-entered three times in an effort to retrieve it. Mr Gilhooley was unmoved by his complaint:

'Ah Mr Gilhooley, ye're a louser! Me pint isn't half finished, and the dogs has bitten the leg off me three times!'

THE job of the publican, although profitable, tends to be a lonely one. He must maintain his dignity and authority at all times, and to achieve this he must never drink with his customers. He must work while others play, and yet like all other mortals he must find time for relaxation and reflection.

Thus, if he wishes to drink he must drink alone, or at least in the company of a few close friends who will provide him with intellectual stimulation worthy of his onerous role in the community.

So, at rare intervals, Mr Gilhooley is conspicuous by his absence from the bar, and it is known that he is in the exalted company of Dr O'Trembler and Myles Grannerty. These absences sometimes last for several days at a time, and it is accepted that serious matters are discussed at these meetings, and that the participants reach Olympian heights of philosophical speculation.

Patrons of Mr Gilhooley's establishment are first made aware that one of these meetings is in progress by the presence of Mrs Gilhooley behind the bar, and the fact that she responds to muffled requests from behind the heavy red velvet curtain which separates the bar from the reportedly sumptuous living quarters of the Gilhooleys by hastily grabbing a fresh bottle of whiskey from the shelf and passing it behind the curtain to the mysterious personage on the other side.

Curious and trivial-minded people have tried to identify the recipient of the bottles over the years, but the most that has ever been seen is a white and bare ankle and a slippered foot disappearing around the edge of the curtain. No one has been able to identify the owner of the foot positively, as Mr Gilhooley has never been see without his highly-polished black boots and thick-knit socks.

These gatherings used to include the illustrious person of one Festus O'Nutty, until Mr O'Nutty departed this life somewhere in his mid-fifties, surrounded by relays of weeping ladies. Most of these ladies were the kind of women whom one would naturally expect to find paying decent respect to a corpse, particularly that of a prominent member of the community, but there was some surprise caused by the presence of a sprinkling of nubile young maidens from the area, whose lamentations were considered tasteless in their intensity and volume, and which led certain uncharitable persons to suggest that 'there was more to the miserable ould fart than met the eye', but it is to be remembered that all great men have their calumniators.

Mr Grannerty was described earlier as having a near-monopoly of trade in the town, and this descripion was given advisedly. Trade in Ballykilferret was dominated by two merchant princes, Mr Grannerty and Festus O'Nutty, until Mr O'Nutty's demise, leaving O'Nutty's General Drapers in the care of his sorrowing widow.

The cause of Festus O'Nutty's death was never clearly established, but the symptoms were severe respiratory difficulties which followed a fall during an evening out with some male friends. It was established that liquor had been consumed by each member of the party, and that various athletic feats of a public house nature had been performed during the evening. But these facts are not sufficient to establish the cause of Mr O'Nutty's demise.

There is an honourable and manly tradition of athletic competition among drinking men in Ballykilferret, which manifests itself in the drinking of pints of stout while the legs of the drinker are held on the bar counter by his fellows and he bends backwards towards the floor, and other practices of a physically stressful nature.

It is known that such feats were performed by Mr O'Nutty on the evening prior to the day of his death, but Mr O'Nutty was renowned for his prowess at these, and had never been known to show adverse reaction to drink or such exertions before.

As Mrs O'Nutty had often said to her women friends in the Total Abstinence Society, Mr O'Nutty was not what you would call a 'drinker', but rather 'a man who took a drink now and then'. Her friends forebore to remark that this 'now and then' included every night of the week.

Be all this as it may, Mr O'Nutty complained of 'flutters in me belly, and wrestler's hould on me heart' on his return from the pub, and immediately took to his bed, calling for the Last Rites. The good woman who finally laid him out hinted that there were signs of a broken collar bone and lacerations to the back of the head, but perhaps it is better to let these musings moulder with Mr O'Nutty in the grave.

It was towards the end of one of Mr Gilhooley's philosophical gatherings that one of those incidents occurred which is welcomed by many as a diversion from the even tenor of everyday life in Ballykilferret.

Seated at the bar in Mr Gilhooley's establishment was an elderly returned exile from the United States, who had been taken there from the parish shortly after his birth to the then housekeeper at the parochial house.

As this gentleman was heard to say that he had been 'twenty-four hours in this goddam country without seeing a single goddam lepreeshan' (it was later thought that the 'lepreeshan' referred to was, in fact, a leprechaun), and there was 'no goddamned action in the godforsaken parish anyway', the curtain behind the bar was thrust aside swiftly to reveal Mr Gilhooley, clad in silk top hat, pink bed jacket of Mrs Gilhooley's with satin bows, long johns, socks and shiny boots.

With an air of great purpose, Mr Gilhooley selected a bottle of his special fifteen-year-old from the shelf, strode around the bar and surveyed his customer from exceedingly close range.

The man tumbled senseless from the stool in the mortal grip of a heart attack, Mr. Gilhooley shook his head rapidly from side to side, drew a deep breath as though summoning his faculties, and stepped unseeing over the corpse which lay with coal-black face upturned, his handsome negroid features already assuming the special dignity of death.

As the Nod Rooney was heard to remark when he surveyed the black man later: 'Be Jasus he got his action all right, even if he didn't see a lepreeshan!'

49

THE widow of Festus O'Nutty was left with the lonely task of rearing their young son, Bagnal, and running the O'Nutty drapery emporium on her own. She showed admirable determination in this, even to the point of refusing Myles Grannerty's graveside offer to take the property off her hands 'for cash' at an appallingly low rate.

Perhaps the burden of her responsibilities made Mrs O'Nutty over-anxious in her approach to the rearing of Bagnal, causing the child to become introvertive, or perhaps there was a susceptibility to the poetic muse somewhere in his genes, but he never showed any aptitude for the running of the business.

His aspirations were artistic ones, and he considered his involvement with O'Nutty's General Drapers a hateful necessity. True, he made various sporadic efforts to bring his own abilities to bear on the business, but these resulted in a series of abject commercial failures.

Evidence of these was a huge pile of garden gnomes stacked against the wall of the back yard, hundreds of pairs of flared jeans and trousers in colours such as gay lilac and orange, which were gathering dust on the shelves of the shop, and football 'nicks which laced up the side as well as football jerseys cut in an off-the-shoulder style.

Bagnal blamed the atmosphere of philistinism in Bally-kilferret for the thwarting of his artistic ambitions. He cited as evidence of this the reaction of Brother Cannabis at the local school to the aforementioned 'nicks and jerseys which he procured for the school team, and the fact that small farmers in the area showed a marked lack of interest in his supply of garden gnomes, which he had thought would provide admirable decorations for their turnip and potato fields.

As Bagnal put it to his friends: ' "Did you design these articles" says he. I thought it was very hurtful to say "articles"; just like that. "I did Brother", says I, real cool like, and lookin' him straight in the eye, and then I looked him up and down slowly, and I went "hmph"! just like that. Oh, he knows where he stands with me ever since!'

And about the garden gnomes: 'Oh, she has me sabotaged all the way. She says the people here has no interest in buyin' gnomes or shrubs. "The end of an old bed to block a gap in a hedge is all they want", she says. But sure, as I told her, it takes time. You have to educate them. It takes time!

'And d'ye know what she said to me? It took time to fill that jug on the mantelpiece to make a doctor out of your brother, and it'll take you only a matter of hours to empty it with your boutiques and your garden centres. Oh she can be very hurtful if she puts her mind to it!'

Bagnal claims that his one bid for independence in attempting to join the Garda Siochana was undermined by the emotional blackmail of his mother, and indeed in fairness to him it must be said that there may be some truth in this, but it must also be stated that his efforts to start modern ballet and mime and movement classes in the training depot in Templemore may not have marked him down as suitable material for an officer of the law.

The most charitable interpretation might be that it was a combination of the ballet classes and his mother's complaints that there would be no one to mind the shop that relegated him to a life of artistic frustration in Ballykilferret.

Bagnal's efforts in the heady realm of theatrical art brought him into direct confrontation with the Canon, and to add to his problems his mother sided with the Church in the Canon's fight against what he described as 'Communist pornography'.

Aware of the prevailing aesthetic climate in Ballykilferret, Bagnal tried hard while casting his plays to anticipate the somewhat predictable objections of the Canon, but it seemed to matter not one whit that Tennessee Williams's *Cat On A*

Hot Tin Roof sported an all-female cast, and that the lady who played the part of the hero, Brick, was well advanced with child.

But the final blow to Bagnal's career as impresario came when the Canon rose to his feet in the auditorium at a production of *The Rose Tattoo,* by the same author, and announced that any man who watched the play 'would grow horns and a tail on him'. One felt from the Canon's manner that, as the direct representative of the Almighty in Ballykilferret, he had a personal discretion to dispense these dreaded appendages.

One thing is sure: there was no man in the audience hardy enough to remain and test the Canon's powers. As the Nod Rooney remarked, 'Sure ye couldn't take the chance. If ye came into Gilhooley's pub with horns and a tail on ye, ye'd never live it down'.

It was after this débâcle that the graffiti began to appear on the walls of the handball alley, and it was these which gave the most hurt to Bagnal, and which caused him the most ostracism. Bagnal could have coped with 'Satan rules O.K.', but 'O'Nutty is a poof' broke his spirit as a theatrical entrepreneur.

Mrs O'Nutty's form of protest against Bagnal's various ventures in the world of art is a subtle one. The decibel level of her breathing increases by several points, and she moves about the shop and house with the sharp angry step of martyrdom. She doesn't speak for days at a time, and eventually retires to bed having announced that she is 'a little depressed'.

The silent war continues until Bagnal weakens enough to enquire whether she would like something to eat. The reply is generally: 'Ah sure what's the use? Sure I'm not long for this world anyway'.

The hunger strike continues until Bagnal capitulates, and then there is a remarkable resurrection. Mrs O'Nutty is up and about and busy as a bee, cleaning, cooking and guarding the morals of Ballykilferret.

It was such a campaign that brought about the disappearance of Bagnal's theatre director's suit of purple velvet and lime-green cowboy boots, and which will be successful, no doubt, in bringing about the disappearance of the safety pins from his nose and ears, which he sports as he tends the O'Nutty delicatessen.

When Bagnal first suggested the idea of the delicatessen he was told the O'Nutty family's image would be destroyed by 'all them flashin' lights and fellas playin' records'.

When it was explained to Mrs O'Nutty that a delicatessen was a place where such things as coleslaw were sold, it became necessary to explain the meaning of the word coleslaw and this resulted in: 'Yer father, God be good to him, didn't build up this business by sellin' cabbage with salad cream on it!'

MENTION has been made of certain incidents which surrounded the proposed visit of an income tax inspector to Ballykilferret. It is to be remembered that Ballykilferret, being basically an agricultural community, did not come within the tax net of inland revenue until recent times, and it is only lightly brushed by the outer meshes even now.

The phenomenon of income tax is new to most people in the area, and thus, like most new phenomena in a remote community, it is viewed with a deal of suspicion.

The reader would be mistaken if he were to conclude that payment of taxes or tithes of any kind was ever made in an open-handed manner by the people of Ballykilferret. The steady inflow of cash to the area for information useful to the ruling powers was never reciprocated by an equally copious outflow.

Indeed, collection of local revenue was always marked by healthy and spirited haggling, which would be taken for granted as the hallmark of thriving commerce in an eastern society. So spirited was the bargaining at times in Ballykilferret's otherwise peaceful history, that the odd landlord's agent was found with the hatchet of disagreement buried deep in his skull. No one was ever brought to trial for these killings, as a strong superstition grew up around their investigation.

It was said that 'anyone enquirin' into them things would have no luck'. And indeed this would seem to have been the case. An unfortunate series of accidents seemed to befall each intrepid investigator, and its gravity appeared to increase in direct proportion to the thoroughness of the investigation, culminating in his death if he pursued his enquiries far enough.

A young and inexperienced investigator was appointed to the area when it was decided to bring the agricultural community within the income tax structure, and showing laudable if naive idealism, he decided to bring the human touch to his work. His first move on taking up the job was to telephone Norbert O'Lunacy at Ballykilferret Farm in the mistaken belief that direct personal contact would eliminate the impersonal and often unfriendly exchange of letters which tends to characterise relationships between revenue officers and the general public.

It was some time before Norbert was able to grasp the fact that he was, in fact, the person required by the caller. He seemed to suffer some mysterious crisis of identity, and even at the end of the conversation the caller was left in doubt as to whether he had been in conversation with Norbert or someone speaking on his behalf.

On enquiring whether he might pay a visit to the farm to interview Norbert, he was told that poison was being laid in the lower field, and that he would come through this field at his peril. When he said that he was prepared to take the risk he was reminded that a previous representative of the Revenue Commissioners had met a horrifying end in similar circumstances in the area, and the fact that the Oireachtas had superseded the British Crown would offer no guarantee that this might not happen again.

When the inspector suggested that he might approach the farm by an alternative route, it was pointed out that this would mean crossing the bottom meadow where the O'Lunacys keep their bull. The inspector said that he was not particularly afraid of animals, but his courage was somewhat shaken by the information that the bull was in a particularly fierce mood.

He was told that if he did not believe this, he might enquire of the veterinary surgeon, but that he would have to hurry because the poor man was 'above in the county hospital', and not expected to last the night.

At this stage the inspector thought that he might try a more devious approach. Perhaps if he were to win the confidence of Mrs O'Lunacy he might gain audience with the elusive personage of Norbert. This was met with the warning that it was 'up to himself' if he wanted to take the risk, but that she had suffered 'one of her turns'.

On expressing his concern for the well-being of Mrs O'Lunacy he was reassured that she was 'alright, but we have her tied up in the haggard at the moment'. It was explained that she had 'bit the leg off the insurance salesman for no reason at all'. It was further explained that she had been 'that way ever since she was bitten herself'.

By now the unfortunate inspector was becoming truly alarmed, and his agitation was only increased by the news that it was thought locally that the cause of Mrs O'Lunacy's condition was rabies because, as it was described to him, 'all the dogs here is gone savage and they're after killin' all the sheep, like, and now they're killin' each other'.

The inspector's concern had now expanded to include such considerations as public health, but his suggestion that the appropriate authorities might be able to catch the marauding animals was met with: 'Ye see they've all run wild, like, and ye wouldn't know where they'd be hidin' out. Ye'd get no warnin', like. They'd be on ye as quick as a cock on a raspberry'.

When he showed further curiosity about the fate of the insurance man, Norbert seemed to have forgotten this earlier reference 'I don't know what ye mean', he said, 'unless ye mean the poor fella they found dead below in the combine harvester'.

It was explained that the ill-fated man had been asking directions in the local pub, where he revealed his identity to the patrons and told them of his mission. They said what this was the last they saw of him until the constabulary found him. The imperfect forensic techniques of the time left some ambiguity as to whether he had received his head injuries before or after entering the combine harvester.

The inspector now retreated to the tried and true defence line of the bureaucrat, the letter, and he was told that Norbert would get it, no doubt, when a replacement had been found for the postman. Apparently the postman had disappeared, and the only trace of him so far was his bicycle, which had been found near the old mine shaft.

The Gardaí had stated that there was evidence that the

unfortunate man had been knocked from the machine because there were signs of a struggle. They could not be sure what had happened until they found the body, but this would take some time as no one knew the exact depth of the old mine shaft, which was probably flooded.

In the meantime, the most they could do was to send the charred remains of some 'Government' envelopes, which had been found beside the bicycle, to the city for further examination.

The conversation concluded with Norbert telling the inspector that he would 'tell the boss ye were callin' when he gets back, whenever that'll be'.

THE traditional attitude of wariness towards visiting minor officials is not confined to matters of revenue. It extends to such people as poultry instructors, and those who perform the necessary and delicate task of artificially inseminating cattle.

The introduction of artificial insemination was the cause of seething prurient curiosity among the young maidens of the locality, the more so because they were unable to satisfy their natural desire for full information on the subject, owing to the reticence of the older generation about such matters.

One unfortunate young lady, a girl of unimpeachable standards of sexual morality, who led the somewhat sheltered life of her profession of piano teacher, ventured to ask her father, a much respected cattle dealer, for some facts about the subject, and was confined to her room without food for three days, so great was the man's shock at his daughter's affrontery.

'We'll have no forty-two-year-old street walkers in this house', he cried as his wife sought to soothe his shattered nerves.

Thus it was that the arrival of the young man who was to perform the first artificial fructifications in the area caused a ferment of interest among the local maidens. To heighten their excitement, he was a powerful young man of handsome, bull-like appearance, with rich black locks and large bovine brown eyes.

It happened that there was a dance taking place in Halla na Seoiníní on the night of the young man's arrival in the town, and he was informed of this by the giggling, broad-hipped and bosomy wench who waited on tables in the local hotel, Bella Donna House. She had been deputed to ensure that the young man would attend the dance for inspection by his potential local harem.

'Ye'll be wantin' to go to the dance, I suppose', she simpered while bending over the table towards him to gather his emptied plate, and presenting her full and rounded breasts for his approval.

'What dance?', he managed to blurt out as he re-moistened his mouth with saliva and tugged his gaze from the warm and inviting cleavage.

"This down at the hall', she replied. 'All the gerrils is dyin' for to have a look at ye. I'd say a fella goin' round doin' your job must be a terrible flirt altogether', and she leaned further across the table and hit him a playful cuff on the side of the head with the effect of blurring his vision so much that he didn't notice the provocative wriggle of her bottom as she flounced from the room, in the kind of mock-indignation which frequently accompanies sexual charades in a rural setting.

By arrangement at the dance there was an unusually large

59

number of 'ladies' choices', and before each of these the young man was beset by struggling groups of young women, each one competing for the pleasure of a dance with him. However, so keen was the competition for his attention, he was unable to cut one out from the herd at the end of the evening. Any girl venturing home with him would have risked everlasting social isolation by her sisters.

But the young man made a mental note that there were easy sexual conquests to be made here if he played his cards correctly.

There were thoughts of pleasurable anticipation on this account running around inside his head as he went about his work the following day, and so absorbed was he by these that he was completely unaware of the row of eyes which peered curiously through the gap of some five or six feet in length, left by the recent removal of a plank high in the wall at the back of the cowshed, as he deftly prepared the seminal appliance.

It was with the same feeling of pleasurable anticipation that the young man swaggered into the Alcatraz Bar, Grill and Chip Shop at the end of his day's labours and surveyed the young ladies and callow youths assembled there, the youths offering no prospect of serious competition.

But it was with complete bewilderment that he found himself ejected into the street by a sudden swarming of angry young maidens who dealt him cuffs, kicks and vicious pinches to the accompaniment of cries of 'ye dirty thing ye! Ye're not wantin' here!' and 'Go 'long to blazes outa' this, ye dirty pervert!'

IN recent years, tourism has played its part in propping up Ballykilferret's ailing economy. In a time when there has been a national effort to systematise this new industry, Ballykilferret has insisted on going its own ingenious way in bringing tourists to the area and keeping them there.

One of the problems of a small town, from the point of view of tourism, is that people tend to dally but briefly, and having spent little or no money they are gone on their way without a backward glance. They buy a packet of cigarettes or an ice cream and this is all the revenue the town derives from their visit.

But Ballykilferret has learned to cope with this problem admirably. There are no signposts outside the town. They were removed by general agreement of the local tourism interests. Thus, the tourist must stop to ask for directions as he leaves the town, and what better men to ask than either of the two old men who are seated on chairs at the roadside on the only two roads leading out of the town? It is here that the ingenious practice of 'givin' the wrong directions' comes in.

Enquiries are met unfailingly with the same set of directions: 'Take the first turn on the right and follow the road around'. This results in their arriving back at the centre of the town again.

The reader might feel that this is a mischievous way to treat a tourist, but he must bear in mind that the tourist is treated to what is described locally as 'a grand drive altogether' out by the canal and the railway bridge, the quarry and the rubbish tip, and by that time they are ready for their lunch at the Alcatraz Bar, Grill and Chip Shop.

It is said by the patrons of this hostelry that it is the one place where you get 'a pile of meat the size of your head', and it is the proud boast of the proprietors that they cut it and cook it on the previous day, and then 'heat it up fresh for the lunch'.

One might imagine that the tourists would be annoyed at being forced to eat in the town against their will, but surprisingly, this is not the case. Ingestion of the fare at the Alcatraz results in a sleepy sensation caused by the heaviness of the food, which tempts the tourists to put off protest to another time.

The sensation might be likened to that experienced by the lotos eaters. As it is said locally: 'Tis grand heavy food. Ye'd hardly keep yer eyes open afther eatin' it'.

Having sloughed off the soporific effects of the Alcatraz menu, the tourists resolve not to be caught so easily again, and head in the other direction out of the town, where once again, owing to the lack of signposts, they are forced to ask directions from an old man seated at the roadside.

He tells them to 'turn sharp right at the forge', which takes them by an unfamiliar lane on to the road they travelled earlier in the day to a spot near the quarry lake, where the old man's nephew is waiting with a flock of sheep across the road. This obstruction causes the tourists to stop and engage in conversation with the nephew, who has never been known to fail to 'make a sale'.

The tourists find that they have rented a boat which they take for a row to the quarry lake, and having proceeded some distance out on the lake, the boat, being leaky, starts to fill, to the consternation of the tourists.

It is then that the nephew plays his master stroke as he gallantly sets out to rescue them in his completely watertight boat.

He generally finds that the tourists will pay anything to be ferried safely to the shore again. They find that they cannot sustain their anger with him because he is 'great crack and would live in your ear'.

The unfortunate tourists have no option but to retrace their journey back from the quarry lake into the town again, where they must find sustenance after their ordeal, and what better place that the one you know already? The Alcatraz Bar, Grill and Chip Shop.

Recovery from the sedative effects of the teatime offerings at the Alcatraz takes until late evening, when it is necessary to find quarters for the night, a need that is admirably filled by Mrs McRobbery's renowned establishment, Bella Donna House, bed and breakfast, (functions in the Salmonella Rooms).

The enterprising characteristics of the McRobberys have been inherited by their daughter, who runs an admirable hair-dressing salon within Bella Donna House. Unfortunately the performance of Ballykilferret's electricity supply is somewhat erratic, and so it is not unknown for a hair-dressing session to have to cease prematurely, leaving the subject with the hair-styling half-completed.

The effects of this are generally so alarming that it is necessary for the customer to remain until electricity supplies have been resumed some time the following day and the session can be completed. So it may be seen that what began as a brief stop for a packet of cigarettes may result in a considerable contribution towards Ballykilferret's exchequer.

THE fact that the dicta of the Nod Rooney are not widely published throughout Ireland is in itself a sad comment on our current set of national values. His immortal 'it takes all types to make a world', or 'Rome wasn't built in a day', would do much to create a climate conducive to moral leadership at a time when our youth is threatened by rampant materialism.

The Nod has a unique capacity for emerging on top from the most complex contretemps. It was he who succeeded in selling a turkey to Norbert O'Lunacy, Ballykilferret's biggest turkey producer, when an unfortunate set of circumstances had brought about an ironic situation where this man was the only person in the town faced with a turkeyless Christmas.

It might be said without any lack of charity that there was a certain amount of poetic justice in this, and I have no doubt that the reader when he learns the facts will agree that Norbert's own avarice and laziness made no small contribution to his misfortune.

The opening scene of this drama is set in Gilhooley's pub, where a stranger approaches Norbert and offers to buy his entire stock of turkeys for cash, at a very competitive price, and to collect them by lorry from the O'Lunacy farm the following day. Norbert is pleased to accept the offer, which spares him the labour of driving the turkeys to the city, and guarantees him a good price.

So pleased is he that he boasts of his bargain to the minor

turkey producers present in the pub, and the Nod Rooney is heard to remark: 'Show us the colour of the man's money and we'll believe ye!'

This elicits an indignant reply from Norbert, who feels outrage at the fact that a man of such miserable aspect with no visible means of support, should comment on a matter of high finance, and indeed the Nod Rooney is suitably humbled when Norbert asks him bitterly: 'What the hell would you know, ye stray oat ye? Sure you haven't the grass of a hen!'

The Nod is humbled even more by the impressive roll of bank notes which Norbert is flourishing in the pub the following night as proof of his business acumen.

Norbert's display of affluence does not extend to buying any of his friends a drink, however, and when he is asked to buy a ticket in the pub's Christmas draw for a turkey, he replies that, as Ballykilferret's biggest turkey producer, 'a turkey is the last thing I'll be needin' this Christmas!', and having chuckled derisively he suggests that the seller should ask the Nod Rooney to buy a ticket.

Now the Nod, having had no employment within living memory, is not noted for his affluence. Indeed you might say that he has never been known to handle actual cash, and yet with the fortunate capacity for survival of his kind, glasses of beer or spirits just seem to materialise in his hand. It has been suggested that he has been guilty of the larceny of the drinks of others, but these allegations should be dismissed as mere attempts by intoxicated persons at character assassination.

Thus with the characteristic fickleness of the mob, cruel attention is turned upon the Nod, and Norbert's diversionary tactic is successful.

The scene is now set in the O'Lunacy farmhouse, where Norbert, upon answering a knock at the door, is confronted by a Garda sergeant and Garda, and in the background is a car with two more men of the ranks in it.

'Did anyone buy turkeys from you?'

'Well, eh, they might have . . . that is . . . they did'.

'Did they pay ye cash for them?'

'Well . . . eh . . . the way it is . . . well they did'.

'Could I see some of the money?'

65

Reluctantly Norbert resorts to his hidden cache for production of same. 'Check them serial numbers, Guard'.

'Begod these is the notes alright, Sergeant. The numbers is here in me notebook'.

'I'll have to take these from ye for examination in the city. I'll give ye a receipt for them, but they'll have to be taken for further examination. We have reason to believe that this is stolen money'.

And the members of the force depart with Norbert's new-found wealth.

The atmosphere in the house is not improved by Mrs O'Lunacy's acid query of: 'Why the hell couldn't ye take the turkeys to the market just like everybody else? Oh no, you had to do somethin' different Mr Onassis!'

Mrs O'Lunacy has an arsenal of punitive sanctions in readiness for times of war between herself and Norbert, and not the least of these is placing an appetising meal before him and then switching the washing machine to 'fast spin'. This results in the food being made inedible by being deluged with plaster from the ceiling, and any protest is met with a long list of repairs which need to be carried out in the house.

Such is the case as Norbert flees his home to the Garda Station in the town to enquire about his money, where he is told by the local sergeant: 'There was none of our lads sent up to your place. I think there's someone afther makin' hare of ye!' The whole ghastly swindle is revealed: confidence man, bogus Gardaí and disappearance of entire turkey stock and money, and Norbert must face the contumely of the habitués of Gilhooley's pub.

To add to the cruel irony of the situation, the winning ticket in the Christmas draw for the turkey is held by the Nod Rooney, although no one can remember his having purchased it. Calumniators are quick to hint that the Nod may have found the ticket on the pub floor or stolen it from someone, but these allegations are most likely born of jealousy at the Nod's good fortune.

This jealousy is further evidenced by the fact that the presentation of the turkey is made in live form, tied to a bit of string, in an effort to bring ridicule upon the winner.

The neurological illness which has earned the Nod his

cruel appellation is very much in evidence as the excitement of his win causes him to shake his head up and down furiously and hop from foot to foot while flapping his arms, and this brings shouts of mock encouragement and jeers from the crowd.

Norbert sees his opportunity to save face, and offers in a condescending manner to purchase the turkey from the Nod, or as he puts it, 'to take it off yer hands'. The Nod is delighted to make a quick sale and to handle the first cash he has ever possessed, and Norbert has solved the problem of procuring a bird for Christmas without facing the ridicule of the town.

'What'll I do with the bird now, Norbert?' asks the Nod.

'Yerra take it up to Brinnse tomorrow', says Norbert, 'but get it to hell out of my sight'.

And so it is that the Nod meets the Canon on his way home from the pub to the little caravan where he lives.

'Good evenin, Nod', says the Canon. 'That is a fine turkey you have there on the string'. (The Canon is a renowned conversationalist.)

'And tell me Nod, where will you keep the bird? Sure you have not the room for it in your small houseen'.

'Ah I'll have to keep it in the caravan alright', says the Nod. 'There'll be room enough'.

'But tell me Nod', says the Canon, 'what about the smell?'

'Ah', says the Nod, 'sure he'll have to get used to that, Canon!'

The Canon goes on his way reflecting that the demands of true witness are high when they necessitate conversation between a man of intellect and such an abject half-wit.

THE fraud perpetrated on Norbert is symptomatic of the regrettable rise in Ballykilferret's crime rate. There was a time when crime was unknown in Ballykilferret, unless you count the disappearance of the odd landlord's agent or tax inspector, but unfortunately the aggression which accompanies extreme materialism throughout the world has reached this hitherto peaceful haven.

Ever quick to spot a business opportunity, Gubnet O'Lunacy was lying in his sleeping bag beside the dying embers of his hearth, a bottle of cheap sherry in one hand and an electronic calculator in the other, when in a moment of inspiration he saw emerging from the area's growth in crime the necessity for a new service industry, and he created Ballykilferret Security to fill this need.

68

It is a modest undertaking, run from a small two-roomed premises in the town, and sometimes manned by Gubnet's nephew, Filbert, when he is home on holiday. The wisdom of leaving Filbert in charge of such a demanding operation might be questioned with some justification.

It wouldn't be unfair to say that he lacks some of the dynamism necessary to run a security firm. Certainly, Mr Grannerty, would be quick to agree with this suggestion.

Recently, he had occasion to telephone the firm to report that his shop was being robbed at gunpoint by three armed men. This information produced great mirth in Filbert, who when he had recovered sufficient breath, remarked that he had often heard of a two-headed calf, but that he had yet to encounter the phenomenon of a three-armed man.

The irate Mr Grannerty was further informed that 'the boss' wasn't there at the time, and he was asked if he could telephone back later at a more convenient time. The information that the boss had gone up to the city with 'Her Ladyship', where 'Her Ladyship' was going to have her hair styled in preparation for her niece's wedding did nothing to relieve Mr Grannerty's anxiety.

Mr Grannerty's frantic attempts to explain further his predicament were interrupted by Filbert's request to him to 'hold on while I get a biro'.

When the conversation was resumed, Mr Grannerty's earnest plea to Filbert to come and give assistance himself was met with the objection that he was 'only mindin' the place', and couldn't leave the premises because an important call might come through and he wouldn't be there to answer the telephone.

Mr Grannerty's blood-pressure was then brought to bursting point by Filbert's request to 'hold on again' because the kettle was on the boil and Filbert wanted to switch it off.

On resumption of the dialogue, Mr Grannerty informed Filbert that the robbers were now threatening to shoot, and he had to explain that it was highly unlikely that the armed men were 'local lads only out for a bit of coddin', even if their faces were covered by nylon stockings.

Filbert pointed out that it was a very difficult feat to get one's head into a stocking. As he phrased it himself, 'it'd cut the nose off ye an' it'd be very itchy too'.

When Mr Grannerty explained that the men's heads were, in fact, covered by ladies' tights, Filbert wanted to know were the 'bum parts' over their faces with 'the legs hangin' down on either side?' because, as Filbert suggested frivolously, 'if they are, they must look right eejits altogether!'

On hearing that the men were emptying the contents of the till into plastic bags, Filbert offered the consoling opinion that they wouldn't get far if the plastic bags were anything like the ones used to hold the waste products of Filbert's place of employment, the Greasy Spoon Café, and Mr Grannerty couldn't see the relevance of the information that Filbert was 'driven mad' by the plastic bags being torn apart too easily by dogs, who spread the rubbish all over the laneway beside the café, leaving Filbert with the unpleasant task of clearing it up.

Mr Grannerty then told Filbert that the robbers were making their getaway in a car, but he couldn't see the relevance of Filbert's next enquiry as to the make of the car used by the robbers until Filbert suggested that if the car was of a certain Japanese make widely advertised on the radio, Mr Grannerty might try to contact the dealer in the area to try and trace the registration.

By now Mr Grannerty was beset by a severe attack of apoplexy, which was not diminished by Filbert wanting to know whether he had thought of 'ringin' the guards'. He explained to Filbert that he had been unable to get a call through to the guards through the exchange, and that it was by the merest chance that he had made contact with Ballykilferret Security, with which, he pointed out, he had binding contract for services.

He further pointed out that the conversation was pointless as the robbers had departed by now, and the life lines on his palms contracted visibly when Filbert replied: 'Ah well then, sure ye've no problem now, so. You're only gettin' yerself all worked up over nothin'. I'll tell the boss ye were ringin' when he gets back, but maybe ye'd like to ring him again yerself. He's a very busy man. It's all go in the security business, ye know'.

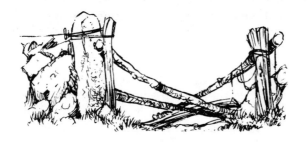

IT has been said that the young men of Ballykilferret have acquired considerable mechanical expertise
through tinkering with car and tractor engines, but the tradition of self-education has not always had the most fortunate
results when extended to the actual operation of vehicles,
although there is a laudable panache about the Ballykilferret
mode of driving.

It was Gubnet O'Lunacy (who else!) who first saw the need
for the founding of a driving school in Ballykilferret to cater
for the peculiarly local needs of drivers.

Mrs Gilhooley was the first woman in Ballykilferret to make
the decision to learn to drive a car. The fact that she did
not actually complete a course of tuition is not relevant to
the decision, and in no way diminishes its value as a mile-
stone in the liberation of ladies in Ballykilferret. The motives
underlying the decision were partly utilitarian and partly
considerations of competitive social status.

She was somewhat taken aback when she learned on making a telephone call to the driving school that 'himself' was
'above at the Cottage Hospital gettin' the head stitched', and
that the training vehicle was 'down at McEnaspic's Garage
gettin' a new front on her afther the accident'.

It was explained that the accident had occurred while
Gubnet was givin 'the bike lesson', which consisted in driving
the car with a number of bicycles tied across the bonnet in
front of the windscreen. This was in preparation for driving
large parties of people home from weddings and funerals,
who had become too intoxicated to ride their machines in
safety, a common occurrence in Ballykilferret.

Gubnet had first realised the necessity for this particular skill while driving home from a wedding some years before.

He was alone at the time, in spite of the fact that the bonnet of the car was festooned with bicycles. This was because his would-be passengers were in a comatose condition following the festivities.

Let me hasten to assure the reader that the coma may not have been the result of over-indulgence in alcohol, and indeed, that there was a suspicion that the salmon course in the Salmonella Rooms was 'off', an allegation hotly denied by Mrs McRobbery, be it said.

Gubnet himself had not consumed what he would consider to be too great a quantity of drink before driving, and it is true that he had avoided spirits, settling for a mere fourteen pints of stout.

It was dark at the time and there was a light rain falling as his vehicle left the road and travelled for a short distance along the grass margin. He was dimly aware of a slight bumping sensation as he travelled along the verge, and of what he described as a sudden flash of light.

His car regained equilibrium and the hard surface of the road, and he drove to the establishment of Mr Gilhooley to ask the favour of one drink to kill the thirst which often occurs some time after consumption of a quantity of stout.

He was admitted and was seated in the after-hours gloom of the bar, shared only with the huddled and unacknowledged figure of the District Justice, sipping the precious fluid, when there was a terrifying and thunderous knock on the front door.

Mr Gilhooley opened it, emboldened by the knowledge that any garda hardy enough to write the District Justice's name in his book risked a posting to Skellig Mor, to be confronted by an enormous itinerant gentleman, who was shaking from head to foot with fright.

'Give us a drink for the love of God mister', begged this towering man of the roads. 'Some bloddy eejit is after drivin' through our camp fire above at the side of the road, and 'tis the mercy of God we're not all killed. If I got me hands on his throat, I'd squeeze 'till he looked his Maker in the face!'

Gubnet was glad that he had parked his car around at the far side of the pub, but somehow his precious last drink had lost some of its savour.

But to return to Mrs Gilhooley; it was explained to her that there was tuition available on the school's curriculum in the techniques required for the driving of certain makes of cars of certain ages. For example, the 1966 Austin Cambridge is a very common vehicle in Ballykilferret, and these vehicles tend to develop wear in the shock-absorbing mechanism after twelve years of hard agricultural use, which is a testimony in itself to the durability of the vehicles.

Thus, the bonnets of these cars tend to point skywards in Ballykilferret, a characteristic which is accentuated by the fact that most of the drivers use them for towing. It will be clear to the reader that it is difficult for the driver to see out over the front, so he must learn to navigate by various local landmarks, such as the tops of trees, familiar telegraph poles or the top of a hill against the sky.

There is even a special course in navigation by the stars for conditions of extreme darkness or elevation of the vehicle's bonnet.

Mrs Gilhooley also learned that there is a special course in what is termed 'the slow look'. This is used when two drivers of tractors with trailers meet on a bend in the road, and one of them alights from his vehicle and crosses the road to chat to the other driver.

It often happens that another vehicle approaches at speed, and that the two tractors with trailers parked on the bend in the road come as a distinct surprise to its driver. This usually results in the newly-arrived car coming to a halt within an inch of the posterior of the party standing in the road.

It is here that the use of 'the slow look' comes into play. It isn't unreasonable to expect that the driver of the vehicle which has been made to halt so abruptly will resort to the use of some abusive language, directed at the man standing in front of him, who must turn with dignity and give him 'the slow look' before resuming his unhurried conversation.

The benefit of the 'slow look' is solely to the deliverer, and derives from the fact that he 'takes nothin' out of himself'. As Gubnet explains to his pupils: 'That's the whole trick of it ye see, ye must take nothin' out of yerself'.

Then there is tuition in the art of driving with dogs in the car; the student is made to drive on a solo trip with two greyhounds aboard, a breed guaranteed to produce the right degree of excitability. At a point along the road a live hare is released, and the greyhounds will then jump on the driver's head, knocking his cap over his eyes.

The driver must master the knack of keeping the vehicle travelling in a straight line while he beats off the animals. The reader will appreciate that this task will be made very difficult by the elevation of the bonnet, which has already necessitated navigation by the stars or treetops.

By this time Mrs Gilhooley was somewhat daunted. She inquired what would be the legal position if a driver were to collide with another vehicle in such circumstances, and was told that there would be no problem if the other vehicle were from outside the Ballykilferret area, because the foreigner would probably require witnesses in order to pursue his case, and the people in Ballykilferret were notoriously 'shy' about appearing in court.

There was one case where a tourist tried to get witnesses to testify against a local man, but their willingness to come forward had more to do with a dispute over a right of way than the actual case at issue, and none of them had actually seen the collision.

As the story is recounted locally: 'Suddenly somethin' made the local witnesses shy, and the foreigner couldn't lay his hands on them at all. One of them was found at the bottom of the quarry cliff. Some said he was pushed, but more said that he must have taken a quare turn in himself and jumped. But sure ye wouldn't mind what people would be sayin' to pass the time.

'The tourist lad? Well he hung around for a long time, but he got no good out of it, and then he went strange in himself and started livin' rough in the woods above on the hill. Ah the people is very kind to him, like. They leaves out scraps for him and that. Ye'll see him dartin' across the road in a set of oul' goatskins now and then if yer headlight beams is at the right angle'.

When Mrs Gilhooley said that she would have to reconsider

the whole idea of having driving lessons, her informant told her that she was 'a terrible woman for changin' her mind'.

It is interesting, if pointless, to note that the rooks in the Ballykilferret area are of a smaller size than those in other areas. Ornithologists believe that this lack of proper development may be brought about by the fact that their roosting periods at night are constantly being disturbed by the headlights of the cars, which rake the sky at almost vertical angles.

Ah well, to quote the Nod Rooney: 'Knowledge is an end in itself'.

How true! How true! For gems of wisdom like this, you must quit the meaningless milling of city throngs, 'leave the Irish sea at yer back at Dublin, head north-west lavin' Lough Owel on yer left', and remember, 'that's the last sea ye'll see 'till ye see Ballykilferret'.